PASTA PLUS

PASTA

Introduced by Luigi Veronelli

Compiled by Simonetta Lupi Vada

PLUS

COLLINS

First published in 1985
by William Collins Sons & Co Ltd
London · Glasgow · Sydney
Auckland · Toronto · Johannesburg

Copyright © 1985 Gruppo Editoriale
Fabbri, Bompiani, Sonzogno, Etas S.p.A.
Milan

Compiler: Simonetta Lupi Vada
Translator: Ros Schwartz
Editor: Nicoletta Flessati

Photographs:
Piero Baguzzi
Alberto Bertoldi
Mario Matteucci
Romano Vada

ISBN 0 00 411213 X

Text set in 'Monophoto' Times
Typesetting by Chambers Wallace, London
Printed and bound in Italy by Fabbri, Milan

CONTENTS

INTRODUCTION   6

WHEAT AND FLOUR   11

COMMERCIAL PASTA   15

HOME-MADE PASTA   21
    Making and Shaping the Dough   21
    Coloured Pasta   27
    Stuffed Pasta   32
    Regional Varieties of Pasta   45
    The Mediterranean Diet   51

ADVICE FROM THE EXPERTS   53
    What Makes Good Pasta?   53
    What Makes a Good Sauce?   53
    The Ten Golden Rules for Cooking Pasta   54
    Hints on Serving Pasta   56
    Sauces for Different Types of Pasta   57
    Can Pasta Be Frozen?   59

PASTA WITH RAGÙ (MEAT SAUCES)   65

PASTA WITH VEGETABLE SAUCES   87

PASTA WITH FISH SAUCES   117

PASTA WITH WHITE SAUCES   131

STUFFED PASTA   149

GNOCCHI   171

PANCAKES   179

INDEX   186

INTRODUCTION

I am a passionate lover of long, twisting, stringy spaghetti, of maccheroni, vermicelli, avemarie, tagliolini, tagliatelle, bucatini . . . and, for me, a book like this is more, much more than merely an invitation to a feast.

What is more, lots of people have been eagerly awaiting this book. Pasta, often referred to by the universally known name of 'spaghetti', is such an 'in' thing that it is of interest to everyone, from the least food-conscious to the most sophisticated palates among us. The truth of the matter is: pasta has conquered the world.

The success of pasta is anything but sudden and is not, therefore, just a passing fad: Alexandre Dumas, who was a great connoisseur of Neapolitan culture from his experiences as one of Garibaldi's Thousand followers, stated more than a century ago that spaghetti was 'a European dish which has travelled with civilization and which, like civilization, is to be found a long way from its cradle'.

That is not all: Giuseppe Prezzolini, a professor at Columbia University, New York, in the 1930s, actually stated, in his *Spaghetti Dinner,* that spaghetti was the American national dish: 'Spaghetti was introduced to the United States by Thomas Jefferson along with poplars from Lombardy, Roman architecture and Tuscan wine. He even imported the first spaghetti machine.'

As if that were not enough, pasta has, in recent years, been loudly hailed as possessing the ultimate virtue. As part of the so-called 'Mediterranean diet', pasta is good for you. It keeps you healthy, young, and may even have aphrodisiac properties!

And so this book is more than welcome. It contains useful background information on types of wheat and flour, looks into commercially produced and home-made pasta (and thankfully returns, inevitably, to the virtues of the home-made). Detailed instructions are included on how to select and combine the ingredients, prepare and colour the dough, roll it out and cut the various pasta shapes.

The regions of Italy

It is a complete and fascinating book which unravels the mysteries of, for example, stuffed pasta, some of the many interesting regional variations in pasta shapes, or the feasibility and methods of freezing pasta (so necessary these days). There is valuable, detailed advice on how to cook and serve perfect pasta and which sauce to choose to complement different pasta types.

Then there are the recipes. So many, and even so, one could go on almost indefinitely, because there are thousands of ways of cooking pasta or, to be precise, ways of combining it with different ingredients and sauces. Here you will find all the best recipes as you are taken on a comprehensive and frenetic journey through Italy. Because there is not one place, from the snowy peaks of the Alps to the sun-baked southern coasts, where you are not offered an age-old traditional dish or some new happy invention of the cook: a plateful of steaming pasta, enlivened with different colours and flavours, depending on local custom. Each one of these recipes provides delightful evidence of the versatility of pasta. Try them out, serve them to your family and friends—and don't forget the wine.

On the subject of wine and pasta, I disagree with three authorities: Alberto Denti di Pirajno, Luigi Carnacina and Mario Soldati. Alberto Denti di Pirajno pronounced: 'After eating pasta with tomatoes, you should not be so profane as to drink wine; on top of pasta and tomatoes, only water should be drunk.' In this instance I support the attitude of the supposedly prejudice-free Venetians when they say: 'The best rule is not to follow any rules.' To my mind, it is water, not wine, that is sacrilegious with pasta and tomatoes. Luigi Carnacina and Mario Soldati advise against drinking wine with pasta either because this is the rule of *grande cuisine* or for dietary reasons (the lipids in the pasta apparently clash with the alcohol in the wine and hamper digestion). That's a lot of nonsense, as an eighteenth-century Sicilian proverb very clearly tells us: *'Voi campari anni e anni? Vivi vinu supra li maccaruni.'* (Do you want to live to a ripe old age? Then drink wine with macaroni.)

Which wine? In my book, there is only one rule that can be applied without exception: the choice of wine is governed by the sauce that accompanies the pasta. Pasta, which is practically inedible on its own, bursts with flavour when accompanied by even the simplest of sauces. By which I mean a few tomatoes, cooked and puréed, or just garlic and oil. It stands to reason that it should be the sauce which governs the choice of wine. With a vegetable sauce, choose a light white or rosé; with a fish sauce, a balanced, dry white wine; for meat sauces, a dry, light red wine; and to accompany game, a dry, full-bodied red wine.

A word of warning: wines should be lighter, younger and fresher than you would choose if you were using the same ingredients—vegetables, fish, meat or game—as dishes in their own right rather than as sauces. The reasons are obvious: the ingredients have been 'diluted' to the consistency of a sauce, the final effect is not so rich, and the flavour is further attenuated by the bland taste of the pasta.

The invitation to a feast is now before you. It is up to you, my reader friend and kindred spirit, to accept, and, having become an expert by attentive reading, to return the invitation.

WHEAT AND FLOUR

Pasta is made from wheat, the most universally cultivated cereal (followed by rice). Not all wheats are suitable for pasta-making, and it is helpful to know why certain wheats are best for its manufacture.

The history of wheat is closely bound up with the history of humanity. Wheat probably developed accidentally from the crossing of wild grass species. It was first cultivated more than 6,000 years ago in Asia Minor and spread to the Middle East and Mediterranean, then to northern Europe and the New World (today the principal producers of wheat).

As the cultivation of wheat spread to areas with different climatic and soil conditions, new varieties developed. Wheat can be divided into two groups: the soft wheats, including the *Triticum vulgare* species, and the hard wheats, which include the species *Triticum durum*. One group of hard wheats known as durum wheats are considered to be the best for pasta-making.

The Structure of the Wheat Kernel

A kernel of wheat is composed of three main parts. The outer covering consists of several layers of fibrous bran. Inside is the germ, or embryo of the new plant. The bulk (80%) of the kernel consists of the endosperm, the starchy food supply for the new plant. Most flour, apart from whole-wheat and brown flours, is the product of the milled endosperm alone.

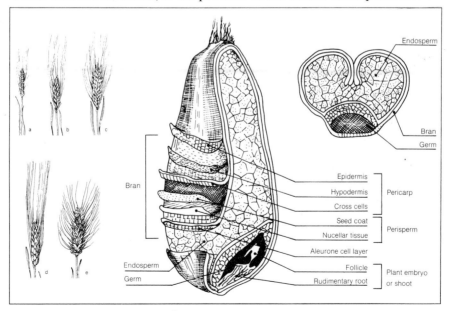

Cross-sections through a wheat kernel

Durum Wheat

There are several varieties of durum wheat within the larger category of the hard wheats. The wheat grain or kernel is very large, often exceeding 1 cm ($\frac{1}{2}$ in) in length. As the name implies, the endosperm of durum wheat is very hard and is pigmented so that it yields an amber-coloured semolina. This colour is reflected in the characteristic amber yellow of pasta. Durum wheat is also high in gluten, an elastic protein with the ability to enclose the starch in flour like a pair of pincers. Taken together, its properties make for pasta that dries easily and holds together well during cooking. Durum wheat is too hard to be suitable for bread-making. It grows best in arid areas and is cultivated extensively in the Mediterranean, the southern U.S.S.R. and parts of Canada and the U.S.A.

The Milling Process

Before it is actually milled, the wheat grain is subjected to a series of wet and dry cleaning processes to extract foreign matter such as dust, grit and straw, and also to eliminate unwanted parts of the grain itself such as the husk and spikes. Simultaneously, conditioning processes regulate the extent to which the grain is dried, in order to improve the quality and yield of the finished product.

After these operations, the milling process begins. This consists essentially of breaking down the grain and the gradual removal of the outer layers of bran. In the first stage of the milling process the grain is crushed between huge rollers. This produces coarse granules. The bran and germ are then separated off by sifting and winnowing in cylinders for that purpose. The 'stripped' endosperm is now a granular meal which is pulverized by further milling and transformed into quality flour. The flour is sifted repeatedly until the required degree of fineness is obtained.

In the production of wholewheat flour, the milling process involves the cleaning, breaking up and grinding of the wheat but the bran and germ are purposely not removed and are present, coarsely ground, in the finished flour. Only flours containing the bran and germ can be termed 'wholewheat' or 'wholemeal' flours. Brown, 'wheatmeal' or 'wheatgerm' flours, on the other hand, are those into which some bran or germ has been re-mixed after milling.

Characteristics of Different Types of Flour

Ordinary flour is the product of soft wheats that have been milled to remove the bran and germ. It is yellowish-white when first milled (the whiteness of commercial flour is the result of subsequent bleaching). It is pleasant to taste and smell and is so fine it is impalpable to the touch. This type of flour is most suitable for making cakes and pastries and has many other culinary uses, for example in sauce-making.

'Strong' or 'bread' flour is a combination of flours milled from hard and soft wheats. It is high in gluten and is therefore good for bread-making. Commercially produced bread is often made from a mixture of soft wheat and hard wheat flours.

Wholewheat flour is coarser than both ordinary and strong flour and is flecked with brown denoting the presence of particles of bran and wheat germ. Because of the fat contained in the germ, this type of flour does not keep as long as the other flours.

For pasta-making at home, the best flours to use are strong or bread flours, or wholewheat flour for making wholewheat pasta. The best commercially produced pasta is always made from milled durum wheat in the form of semolina, that is, coarsely ground meal, rather than more finely ground flour. This is because flour in the granular form of semolina absorbs less water than finer flour and will dry more quickly. Although semolina can be bought in packets for use at home, it is not usually used to make home-made pasta. Pasta made at home is, after all, fresh pasta and does not need to have good drying or long-keeping qualities. Strong or bread flour is perfectly satisfactory for home pasta-making.

The different types of flour vary in nutritional content. This is related to the nutrients contained in the various parts of the wheat kernel: the bran, germ and endosperm. Flour made from endosperm alone will contain about 70% of the protein present in the original grain and some vitamins of the B complex. As a starch food it is predominantly a form of energy. Extra vitamins and iron are often added to flour after milling. However, ordinary flour contains little dietary fibre. Wholewheat flour, from which nothing has been removed, contains all the carbohydrate, protein and vitamins originally present in the grain of wheat (apart from a small percentage lost during processing). In addition, the cellulose material in the bran provides a valuable amount of fibre.

COMMERCIAL PASTA

Pasta is obtained from the processing of wheat flour. Its origins are extremely ancient: they go back as far as the Etruscans who are said to have made the first lasagne. The use of pasta spread across Italy from the fourteenth century onwards and it was at the beginning of the nineteenth century that the first simple pasta machines appeared in Naples. Nowadays, modern technology has made it possible to standardize the production processes, and pasta factories are to be found all over Italy and in other countries too.

The Ingredients

Commercial pasta is made from two basic ingredients: flour and water. The flour must be from hard grain, and preferably durum wheat, suitably milled and sifted. The protein-rich part of the flour, known as *gluten,* is very important, as this is the ingredient which makes the pasta cohere. The other ingredient, water, must also be chosen accurately; it is best if the water is medium hard. For egg pasta and the so-called 'special' pasta, other ingredients are required, as described on page 16.

The Production of Dried Pasta

The flour and the water are combined in a machine called a press. The kneading process follows. The dough is then drawn out and passed through various dies or forms which determine the shape and appearance of the finished product. Just some of the shapes obtained from drawing the dough through these dies are spaghetti, smooth tagliatelle (noodles) and scalloped tagliatelle, farfallette (butterflies or bows), quadrucci (squares), rigatoni (fluted tubes), smooth penne (quills) and fluted penne, lingue di passero (very thin noodles), and capelli d'angelo (very thin spaghetti).

Dried pasta shapes are divided into two main categories: *pasta asciutta,* for cooking in water and eating with sauces, and *pasta in brodo,* smaller shapes for cooking in a broth or soup. For all these types of pasta, the texture of the surface is important as the pasta must be able to absorb sauces and seasonings yet stand up well to cooking.

After the drawing-out stage, the pasta is in its final shape but still contains about 30% too much water and so will not keep well. The

Fresh egg pasta (here, long maccheroni)

water content has to be reduced to about 12.5%, a process that involves various delicate drying stages. Next, the pasta needs a 'maturing' period during which it becomes stable. It must remain for a time in the air-conditioned environment where it was produced as a sudden change in temperature could cause it to deteriorate.

Packaging is the last stage in this series of operations. Pasta is packaged in cellophane packets or cardboard boxes.

Italian Pasta Regulations

Three types of pasta are covered by these regulations: dried pasta, fresh pasta and special pasta. The production process described above applies to dried pasta, which is by far the main form in which pasta is sold. Under Italian law, dried pasta must be made solely from hard wheat flour and water.

Soft wheat flour is allowed in the making of fresh pasta but it is forbidden to add any organic or inorganic substance, as for other types of pasta, except those authorized by the regulations on special pasta.

Special pasta includes pasta made with egg, green pasta made with spinach, pasta with fillings, wholewheat pasta and pasta that has been enriched or reduced in some way. For pasta made with egg, the law in Italy provides for a ratio of 4 whole hen's eggs to every 1 kg ($2\frac{1}{4}$ lb) of flour, for both dried pasta and fresh pasta. For other special types of pasta dehydrated or concentrated tomato, nutmeg, extra gluten and malt may all be used. Wholewheat pasta comes under the heading of health food and has special provisions.

Pasta Guidelines in the U.K.

Although half the pasta consumed in the U.K. is still imported from Italy, good-quality pasta is also manufactured in Britain. (Britain actually exports wholewheat pasta to Italy!) The code of practice of the Food Manufacturers' Federation in Britain stipulates that all dried pasta products for sale to the consumer should be made from hard wheat and/or durum wheat. Egg pasta should contain 135 g ($4\frac{1}{2}$ oz) of hen's eggs (approximately 2 to 3 eggs) to every 1 kg ($2\frac{1}{4}$ lb) of flour.

Characteristics of Good Dried Pasta

Good dried pasta made from durum wheat is a distinctive amber yellow colour, has a smooth surface and is free from specks. It is hard, but not too brittle. Good pasta is also initially 'resistant' to cooking and does not lose its shape or become mushy. It remains firm, hence the expression *al dente* for pasta that is done but still chewy to the bite. It should double in volume during cooking. Dried pasta made from soft wheat, on the other hand, breaks easily, has a dull, chalky colour and specks. It does not keep its shape so well during cooking and may become sticky, while the cooking water may become cloudy with excess starch.

The Different Types of Commercial Pasta

There is a pasta to suit all tastes and every occasion. Here is a selection of commercial pastas.

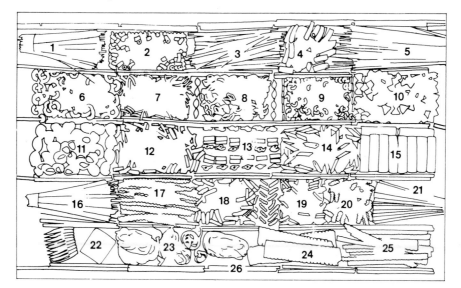

1. Wholewheat bucatini
2. Ditalini, tubetti, maccheroncini
3. Spaghetti
4. Maccheroni, maniche di frate
5. Wholewheat spaghetti
6. Creste
7. Sedanini, gramigna gigante
8. Lumachine
9. Sedani ritorti, gobbetti
10. Farfalle, galoni
11. Lumaconi, chiochiole
12. Wholewheat maccheroni
13. Marille, maccheroni
14. Maltagliati, penne
15. Cannelloni
16. Bigoli
17. Fusilli lunghi
18. Fusilli corti, viti
19. Green fusilli corti, viti, delizie
20. Reginelle, pappardelle
21. Trenette, bavette
22. Lasagne, dolari
23. Tagliatelle, fettucce, lasagnette, lagane, laganelle, tagliatelline
24. Pappardelle
25. Pappardelle, mafaldine
26. Zite, maccheroni lunghi

Different types of commercial pasta (see overleaf)

HOME-MADE PASTA

MAKING AND SHAPING THE DOUGH

The term *pasta casalinga,* as fresh pasta is called in Italy, generally means pasta made with egg, flour and, sometimes, olive oil. There are other types of pasta made with flour from different kinds of cereal, and mixed only with water.

The Utensils

To prepare egg pasta the authentic way, you require only a few utensils, but they should have specific characteristics. First of all, you need a wooden pastry board, which should be long and wide and perfectly smooth, with no knots or joins. Alternatively, a marble slab may be used, but a wooden board is better as it enables you to roll out the dough into a very thin sheet, and the wood absorbs any excess moisture from the dough while the pasta is being kneaded. Another essential piece of equipment is a long wooden rolling pin (traditionally made of cherry wood and as smooth as a looking-glass). Its size is also important: it should be 4 to 5cm ($1\frac{1}{2}$ to 2in) in diameter and at least 1 metre (3ft 3in) long so that the dough can be wrapped round it and turned without hanging over the ends of the pin and breaking off.

You also require a fairly short, flexible, metal spatula to lift the dough from the pastry board, a serrated or smooth wooden pastry wheel, and a very sharp, wide-bladed knife to cut the dough into various shapes.

Pasta-Making Machines

Nowadays, the rolling pin has been replaced by either manual or electric pasta machines for rolling out the dough. The most recent electric machines enable you to go from the raw ingredient stage to cutting out the shapes in next to no time. The manual machine is more common because it costs less and is easy to use. It has smooth rollers to stretch the pasta into a sheet and ridged rollers to cut the rolled-out dough into tagliatelle (noodles) and tagliolini (thin noodles). The sheet of dough can be made even finer by adjusting the distance between the two smooth rollers. The rollers are turned by means of a handle at the side.

Ingredients for home-made pasta (here, fettuccine, tagliatelline, quadrettini, farfalle)

The electric pasta machine works in the same way but is operated by a motor. With an electric pasta machine, all you have to do is put the ingredients (following the quantities given in the instruction booklet or recipe) into the appropriate containers, close the lid tightly and press the button. A series of small blades rotate slowly, mixing the ingredients to a compact and perfectly smooth dough which is ready to be shaped in various ways. Other mechanical and electric appliances have little plastic or stainless steel discs through which the pasta is drawn to obtain the various shapes.

Various machines are on the market with different features. It is worth investing in one of the more sophisticated machines if you make large quantities of pasta often. (The larger machines work best with substantial amounts.) Otherwise you may want to experiment at first with the simple and efficient manual pasta machine, or make the pasta entirely by hand, as set out below.

Choosing the Ingredients

To return to home-made pasta, there is basically one way of making pasta with flour and eggs, that is, plain egg pasta without extra colouring or flavouring ingredients. For home-made pasta the proportions are 1 egg to every 100 g (3½ oz) of flour, or 7 eggs to every 1 kg (2¼ lb), a pinch of salt and a little olive oil to soften the dough (but this is optional). You can always replace the eggs with water but the pasta will not be so flavoursome.

You can use white flour, strong or bread flour or wholewheat flour. It is a good idea to sift white flour to eliminate any lumps. Do not use very old flour as its quality will have deteriorated.

The eggs must be very fresh and cold, but not straight out of the refrigerator. They should be kept in a well-ventilated room, where the temperature is constant at around 7° to 13°C (45° to 55°F), or in the least cold part of the fridge. Excessive heat or excessive cold can have an adverse effect on the basic ingredients and on the texture and elasticity of the dough itself.

Use only the freshest eggs to make the best home-made pasta. Here's a useful tip for testing the freshness of an egg. The fresher the egg, the smaller the volume of air in the air pocket at its broader end. Immerse the egg in salt water (about 60 g [2 oz] salt to 1 litre [1¾ pints] of cold water): a fresh egg will sink to the bottom, not-so-fresh eggs will hover above the bottom and eggs which are more than a month old will float upwards (see the diagram below). To make doubly sure, it is better to break the egg into a bowl first: if it is fresh, the yolk will be full with a convex shape while the white will be very elastic.

Mixing the Dough

Heap the flour in a mound and make a hollow in the centre. Break the eggs into the hollow and add a little olive oil (if you are using oil) and

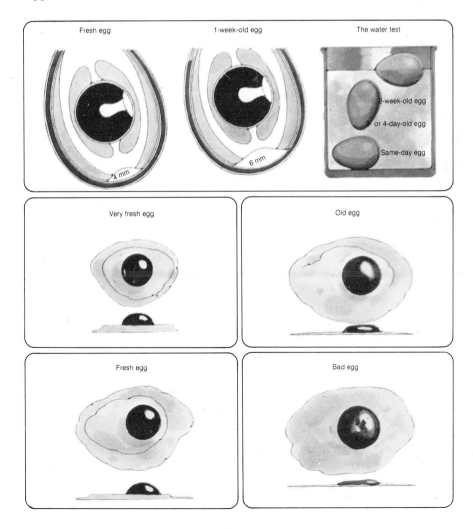

How to test the freshness of an egg

a pinch of salt. Begin to work the eggs into the flour, carefully, with your fingertips. When the flour has been completely absorbed by the eggs, knead the dough with both hands for 10 to 15 minutes until it is firm, smooth and elastic. While you are kneading the dough, it is a good idea to flour your hands from time to time as you stretch the dough and fold it back on itself over and over again. Little bubbles will form on the surface indicating that the dough is sufficiently kneaded. At this point, gather the dough into a ball, dust it with a handful of flour and put it in a lightly floured bowl. Cover with a cloth and let it rest for about 15 minutes.

How to Roll Out the Dough by Hand

To roll out the dough evenly, first flatten it with the palm of your hand, then continue to flatten the dough with the rolling pin, working vigorously from the centre outwards, in all directions, so that the dough becomes more or less circular and the same thickness all over. To turn the sheet of dough without breaking it, wrap it around the rolling pin and rotate dough and pin gently on the pastry board. When the dough is too unwieldy to be wrapped round completely, repeat the operation but only wrap one edge round the rolling pin, letting the rest fall on to the pastry board; the edges will become very thin from the action of the rolling pin while the sheer weight of the sheet of dough will stretch the centre. By the end of the process, the sheet of dough should be about 2 mm (1/10 in) thick.

How to Roll Out the Dough by Machine

After mixing and resting the dough, you can speed up the kneading process by using a manual pasta machine. The resulting sheet of dough will not be quite as thin nor have such a fine texture as hand-rolled dough.

The machine kneading process is simple: a piece of dough is passed five or six times through the rollers, set at the maximum distance apart; each time the dough is folded back on itself and a different end is fed into the machine first. Then the distance between the rollers is reduced by turning the appropriate knob and the dough is passed through several times more. The rollers are adjusted until the desired thickness of dough is reached.

How to Make the Different Shapes

To cut the sheet of dough by hand, you will need, as already mentioned, a heavy knife with a very sharp, wide blade. Leave the sheet of dough on the pastry board to dry for a short while, though not too long or the pasta will dry out too much and break.

Tagliatelle or Fettucce

To make tagliatelle or fettucce, roll the sheet of dough up into a long narrow sausage. Then cut strips 1 cm ($\frac{1}{2}$ in) wide and unroll each coil by hand, separating the noodles on the pastry board to allow them to dry out.

Tagliatelle are generally served with a vegetable sauce or with any kind of ragù (a meat sauce such as Bolognese sauce).

Fettuccine, Linguine, Lagane or Laganelle

Proceed as for tagliatelle but make the strips about $\frac{1}{2}$ cm ($\frac{1}{4}$ in) wide.

Serve with butter and cheese, with cream or with béchamel sauce.

Tagliatelline, Tagliolini or Taglierini

Proceed as for tagliatelle but cut the strips very fine, about 2 to 3 mm ($\frac{1}{10}$ to $\frac{1}{8}$ in) wide. Try not to squash the roll of dough as you make clean, sharp cuts. Unroll each coil as soon as you have cut it as it will tend to stick together.

Serve with meat broth, but also excellent with cheese and butter or with a fresh tomato sauce.

Maltagliati

The dough is rolled up as for tagliatelle and the same sharp wide-bladed knife is used. This time, cut zig-zag strips about 1 cm ($\frac{1}{2}$ in) wide: you will end up with irregular diamond-shaped pasta shapes—hence the name maltagliati which means 'badly cut'.

Maltagliati are usually cooked in vegetable soup, especially with chick-peas or beans.

Quadrettini or Quadrucci

Roll the dough up in the usual way. Cut strips about 1 cm ($\frac{1}{2}$ in) wide, then turn each rolled-up coil round and cut it across into little pieces about 1 cm ($\frac{1}{2}$ in) long. This will give you little squares that should be separated immediately and left to dry on the pastry board.

Cook in meat or vegetable broth.

Pappardelle or Reginette

Leave the dough rolled out in a thin sheet. Using a serrated wooden pastry wheel, cut the dough into long strips 2 to 3 cm ($\frac{3}{4}$ to $1\frac{1}{4}$ in) wide.

Serve with rich meat sauces (especially those made with game or giblets) or with mushrooms.

Farfalle, Nodini or Galani

Again starting with the sheet of dough, and before it has become too dry, use the serrated wooden pastry wheel to cut horizontal strips 1 to 2 cm ($\frac{1}{2}$ to $\frac{3}{4}$ in) wide (depending on whether you intend to cook the shapes in soup or for a main course). Then, without moving the strips, make vertical cuts 4 to 5 cm ($1\frac{1}{2}$ to 2 in) apart: this will give you rectangles which you pinch in the centre to create the distinctive butter-fly shape.

Depending on the size of the farfelle, serve with tomato sauce, Bolognese sauce, with the juices from roast meat or stews, or in vegetable soups.

Lasagne

Using either the knife or the wooden pastry wheel, cut strips about 8 to 10 cm (3 to 4 in) wide from the sheet of dough. Cut these strips into rectangles or squares of the required length.

Classically lasagne is baked in the oven with a very rich Bolognese sauce and a béchamel sauce, or is used to make cannelloni shapes which are then stuffed with meat, ricotta and green vegetables, or cheese and ham.

Pasta Grattugiata or Pasta Tritata

Mix the pasta dough as described but add a little more flour to give it a firmer consistency. After kneading and resting the dough divide it into pieces and roll each piece into a ball. Grate each ball against a metal grater, letting the flakes fall on to the floured pastry board. Allow them to dry thoroughly before cooking.

Grated pasta is best cooked in meat or vegetable broths.

COLOURED PASTA

Coloured pasta is prepared in the same way as plain pasta with a slight modification of the basic ingredients (flour and eggs) and the addition of other ingredients which not only colour the pasta but give it a different flavour.

The dough must be coloured only with natural ingredients carefully measured, depending on the colour you wish to obtain. Certain ingredients, like cocoa, saffron and paprika, should be added to the dough in tiny amounts because their flavour must not become overpowering.

Green Pasta, Made with Spinach

For every 400 g (14 oz) flour, allow 200 g (7 oz) fresh spinach, 3 eggs and a pinch of salt. Wash the spinach and boil it without adding any water, only a pinch of salt. Let the spinach cool and squeeze it out by hand before putting it through a vegetable mill. Add the spinach to the flour and eggs and make the dough as described earlier. If the spinach has retained too much moisture you may need to add a little more flour. Then roll out the dough and cut out the required shapes. Green pasta is slightly less elastic than plain pasta and the sheet of dough will not be so transparently thin. It is advisable to divide it into several pieces and roll them out one at a time, covering the others with a tea-towel to prevent them drying out.

Sea-Green Pasta, Made with Mint

For every 400 g (14 oz) flour, allow a large handful of fresh mint, 2 eggs and a pinch of salt.

Boil the mint with a pinch of salt, drain, and dry it thoroughly with kitchen paper. Put it through a sieve. Add the mint to the other ingredients with a little water or milk (about 2 tablespoons) if the eggs are not sufficient to bind the flour. Roll out the dough and cut out tagliatelle about $\frac{1}{2}$ cm ($\frac{1}{4}$ in) wide. Mint pasta can be served with butter and cheese, or with fresh cream and cheese.

Grey-Green Pasta, Made with Nettles

For every 400 g (14 oz) flour allow 100 g ($3\frac{1}{2}$ oz) fresh nettles, 3 eggs and a pinch of salt.

Wash the nettles carefully. Boil the leaves with a pinch of salt, drain, and dry them well and put them through a sieve. Add the nettles to the other ingredients with a little water if the eggs are not sufficient to bind the flour. Roll out the dough and cut out tagliatelle 1 cm ($\frac{1}{2}$ in) wide.

Beige Pasta, Made with Mushrooms

For every 400 g (14 oz) flour, allow 50 g (2 oz) dried cep mushrooms, 3 eggs and a pinch of salt.

Soften the mushrooms by soaking them in a little warm water for a few minutes. Drain, reserving the water, and fry the mushrooms gently in oil with a little white wine and stock. Cook until the mushrooms are soft and the liquid has completely evaporated. Put the mushrooms through a sieve and mix the purée with the other ingredients, adding a few teaspoonfuls of the water the mushrooms soaked in (strain it first). Add more flour to obtain a fairly firm dough. Roll out the dough as thinly as possible and cut into your favourite shape.

Yellow Pasta, Made with Pumpkin

For every 400 g (14 oz) flour, allow 400 g (14 oz) pumpkin and 2 eggs.

Cut the pumpkin into slices, peel them and discard the seeds. Bake until tender in the oven (you can also boil the pieces in salted water but the pumpkin will retain more moisture). Put the pumpkin through a vegetable mill. If the purée is too liquid, dry it out gently in a saucepan over a low heat, stirring continuously. Add it to the other ingredients and make the dough as described earlier, again, with more flour if necessary.

Different types of coloured pasta

Orange Pasta, Made with Carrots

For every 400 g (14 oz) flour, allow 250 g (9 oz) of young sweet carrots, 3 eggs and a pinch of salt.

Scrape the carrots, top and tail them and steam or boil them in a little lightly salted water. Drain and put through a vegetable mill. If the purée is too liquid, heat in a saucepan over a very low heat. Continue as for yellow pasta.

Red Pasta, Made with Tomatoes

For every 400 g (14 oz) flour, allow a spoonful of concentrated tomato purée, 4 eggs, and salt.

Proceed as for plain pasta adding the tomato purée to the eggs before mixing them with the flour. To obtain a brighter colour, add more tomato purée.

Purple Pasta, Made with Beetroot

For every 400 g (14 oz) flour, allow 1 large cooked beetroot, 2 eggs and a pinch of salt.

Peel the beetroot, cut the flesh into small pieces and put through a vegetable mill, letting the purée fall into a dish lined with muslin. Bring the edges of the muslin together and squeeze the excess juice out of the beetroot. Then add the purée left in the muslin to the flour, eggs and salt and proceed as usual. The amount of flour can be varied depending on how much beetroot purée is obtained. This pasta is not particularly elastic and cannot be rolled out very thin.

It is advisable when cutting the sheet of dough to sprinkle it with a little cornmeal or fine semolina to make it easier to roll up. It is best to work quickly because purple pasta soon dries out.

Brown Pasta, Made with Cocoa

For every 400 g (14 oz) flour, allow 60 g (2 oz) unsweetened cocoa and 4 eggs. You can add less cocoa if you prefer a lighter pasta with a less pronounced flavour. Follow the same procedure as for plain pasta, adding the sieved cocoa to the flour.

This particular type of pasta is for serving with game, pigeon or duck.

Bright Yellow Pasta, Made with Saffron

For every 400 g (14 oz) flour, allow a sachet of saffron, 4 eggs and a pinch of salt.

Crumble the saffron and dissolve it in a very little warm water. Add the solution to the eggs in the centre of the mound of flour and proceed as for plain pasta.

White Pasta, Made with Cheese

This type of pasta is called 'white' to distinguish it from plain pasta. In fact it has a yellow colour because of the eggs, but it is a pale, faded yellow that is very nearly white.

For every 200 g (7 oz) flour, allow 200 g (7 oz) Parmesan cheese and 3 eggs. Grate the cheese very finely and add it to the flour, then add the eggs and proceed as for plain pasta.

This type of pasta cannot be kept long because of its cheese content. It is very tasty and therefore requires a simple, delicately flavoured seasoning, such as fresh melted butter or a tomato sauce.

Blue Pasta, Made with Liqueur

For every 400 g (14 oz) flour, allow 2 eggs, a little water and 8 teaspoons of blue Curaçao.

Add the water and the liqueur to the flour and eggs and mix to a fairly firm dough. Continue to make the pasta as described before. For a clearer blue colour, use only the whites of the eggs and add more water.

This type of pasta, with its distinctive colour and flavour, should be served with a delicately flavoured white sauce, butter and cheese or cream and cheese.

Pink Pasta, Made with Tomatoes and Cream

For every 400 g (14 oz) flour, allow about $\frac{1}{4}$ litre (9 fl oz) single cream, 1 teaspoon of concentrated tomato purée (use the variety sold in tubes) and 2 eggs. Mix the tomato purée with the cream and add to the flour and eggs. Proceed as for plain pasta.

Rosy Pasta, Made with Strawberries

For every 400g (14oz) flour allow 100g (3½oz) strawberries, 3 eggs, a pinch of salt and a little milk or single cream.

Purée the strawberries in a liquidizer or by pressing them through a nylon sieve. Add the strawberry purée to the flour, eggs, salt and a little milk or cream. If the dough is too wet, add a handful of flour. Then roll out the dough, which tends to be delicate, twice, into a sheet that is not too thin, and cut thin fettuccine.

You are advised to eat strawberry pasta at once and serve it with a white sauce with a cream and cheese base or simply with melted butter and Parmesan cheese.

Black Pasta, Made with Cuttlefish Ink

This type of pasta is grey rather than black because the eggs tone down the strong black of the ink. For every 400g (14oz) flour allow the ink of 3 or 4 cuttlefish, 3 eggs and a little water.

Dissolve the cuttlefish ink, which is contained in a sac inside the mollusc, in a little cold water and add to the flour and eggs. Add enough water to make a medium firm dough. Roll out the dough as thinly as possible, adding flour if necessary, and cut out the required shapes. This type of pasta is only served with fish sauces made with cuttlefish, squid, or shellfish, and so on, and without cheese. You can add more flavour by sprinkling over chopped fresh herbs just before serving.

STUFFED PASTA

Stuffed pasta includes all the different types of pasta which have some kind of filling – whether meat, vegetables, cheese or fish – and which vary in shape and size according to the culinary traditions of the different regions of Italy. Stuffed pasta is served on its own, with sauces or in broth.

Meat stuffings are made with beef, veal, pork or turkey, usually minced, cooked and mixed with ham, mortadella or another type of

Agnolotti with Tomato Sauce

sausage, or with giblets. Meat-based fillings are usually flavoured with spices, cheese and egg, which also helps to bind the stuffing.

Then there are fillings made from meat and vegetables or vegetables and cheese. Among the most commonly used vegetables are spinach, chard, asparagus, lettuce and pumpkin. Breadcrumbs mixed with cheese and sausage make an economical filling, and there are stuffings containing fish or fish mixed with boiled vegetables.

Depending on their shape, filling, and region of origin, the stuffed pastas have different names: agnolini, agnolotti, ravioli, cappelletti, tortellini, calzoncini, rotoli (rolls) and cannelloni. All these preparations take time to make which is why it is advisable to prepare the stuffing in advance and to have the appropriate utensils.

As well as the usual pastry board and rolling pin, or pasta machine to save time and effort, you will also find the following useful: a serrated or smooth pastry wheel, a very sharp knife, round and square moulds, and, for certain dishes like cannelloni, lasagne, and pancakes, a range of ovenproof dishes.

Agnolini and Agnolotti

Agnolini are a speciality of Mantua in Lombardy and agnolotti come from Piedmont.

Stuffings for agnolini vary from city to city and even from one family to another. Agnolini can be served simply with butter and cheese or with top of the milk and cheese, or they can be cooked in a beef or chicken broth.

To prepare agnolini: mix the dough using the same proportions of flour and eggs as in the basic recipe for plain pasta (page 22). It is a good idea to make the dough a little softer so add a little water if necessary. Roll out the dough very thin. Try to work in a cool but draught-free room to protect the dough from drying out before it is stuffed and shaped. As soon as the dough has been rolled out, use the pastry wheel to cut the dough into squares each measuring about 3×3 cm ($1\frac{1}{4} \times 1\frac{1}{4}$ in) for the agnolini and 6×6 cm ($2\frac{1}{2} \times 2\frac{1}{2}$ in) for the agnolotti. Take a small quantity of stuffing and place it in the centre of the square, then fold the corners together to make a triangle. Press the edges together so that the dough adheres perfectly. This ensures that

Tortellini in Cream with Vol-au-Vent

the stuffing will not come out during cooking. At the same time, wrap the pasta round your forefinger, overlapping and joining the two opposite corners. While you are doing this, the third corner will fold under by itself.

Agnolini and agnolotti can also be made from round shapes. To make these, cut discs from the sheet of dough and proceed as described above.

Calzoncini or Casonsei

Calzoncini are a kind of large ravioli, a typical pasta from Brescia in Lombardy, and consist of half-moon shapes filled with bread soaked in milk and mixed with sausage and cheese. They are served with melted butter and Parmesan cheese (see recipe page 159).

To prepare calzoncini: make the usual egg pasta dough and roll it out into a thin sheet. Then cut rectangles each measuring about 7.5 × 12 cm (3 × 5 in). Put a mound of stuffing in the centre of each rectangle and fold the dough lengthways. Press the sides down around the stuffing then, holding the edges of the rectangle with your fingers, pull the edges down to give the ravioli the shape of calzoncini.

Cannelloni

Cannelloni are little rolls of pasta stuffed with meat or with a mixture of green vegetables and ricotta, or with slivers of ham and cheese. They are eaten all over Italy, from the north to the south.

To prepare cannelloni: make the usual egg pasta dough and roll it out into a fairly thin sheet. Cut out large squares or rectangles. Lay the filling on one half of each square and roll the dough into a tube shape over the filling. Cannelloni are cooked in the oven with a béchamel or tomato sauce, a Bolognese or other meat ragù or with a velouté sauce.

Marubini

A round variety of ravioli which is typical of the Lombardy town of Cremona, marubini are filled with stuffings made from minced beef, veal, pork sausage or brains, with Parmesan cheese, egg and spices. They are cooked in meat broth and served with Parmesan. They can

Ravioli with Marrow Filling and Ragù

also be served on their own, drained, with the sauce of your choice (see recipe page 161).

To prepare marubini: make the usual egg pasta dough and divide it into two equal parts. Roll out into two thin sheets. Place little mounds of filling on one sheet, 2 to 3 cm ($\frac{3}{4}$ to $1\frac{1}{4}$ in) apart, and cover with the other sheet of dough, pressing the edges tightly together.

After pressing down the dough around each mound of filling, use a serrated or smooth pastry cutter to cut out the marubini. Then lift away the leftover dough which can be cut in tiny pieces and cooked in a vegetable soup.

Ofelle

These are a square sort of ravioli from the Friuli-Venezia Giulia region and are stuffed with spinach, veal and sausage. They are served with butter and Parmesan cheese (see recipe page 162).

To prepare ofelle: mix the flour with some potato purée, eggs, yeast (to lighten the dough) and salt to obtain a dough rather like that used to make potato gnocchi (dumplings). Then roll out the dough as thinly as possible (it is very fragile and you will not be able to roll it out as thinly as the ordinary flour and egg dough). Cut the dough into squares measuring 6 to 7 cm ($2\frac{1}{2}$ to 3 in) and put the stuffing on half the squares. Cover with the remaining squares, pressing the pasta down firmly to seal in the filling.

Panciuti or Pansoti

These are fat or bulging ravioli, and are a typical pasta from Genoa in Liguria. They are triangular or round in shape and are stuffed with a filling of cheese, eggs and herbs. In the classic Ligurian recipe they are served with a sauce made from pounded walnuts, pine nuts and bread diluted with milk and olive oil (see recipe page 162). They are also good with melted butter and cheese.

To prepare panciuti: make the dough with flour, water and white wine (using more water than wine) to obtain a medium firm consistency. Roll out the dough in a thin sheet and cut out triangles with sides 6 to 7 cm ($2\frac{1}{2}$ to 3 in) long, or discs with a diameter of about 6 to 7 cm ($2\frac{1}{2}$ to

Panciuti with Melted Butter and Cheese

3 in). As you cut out the shapes, keep them covered with a cloth to stop them drying out. Then fill each triangle or disc with the prepared stuffing and fold over the edges, making sure you seal them tightly.

Pasta Piena

This is a sheet of pasta stuffed and cut into small squares and is a speciality of the Romagna region. The stuffing is usually made from beef marrow, ham, Parmesan cheese, breadcrumbs, spices and egg. The traditional recipe, however, has a simpler filling of soft cheese, Parmesan, egg and salt.

The pasta is cooked in good meat broth and accompanied by grated Parmesan cheese (see recipe page 164). If you prefer, you can drain off the broth and serve the pasta with the sauce of your choice.

To prepare pasta piena: make egg pasta dough and roll it out as thinly as possible. Then cover half the sheet of dough with the stuffing, evening it out with a long spatula. Fold over the other half of the dough and seal the edges tightly. Press a little with the rolling pin to make the two layers of dough stick together.

Using a pastry wheel, cut strips about 2 cm ($\frac{3}{4}$ in) wide then cut across the strips to make little squares.

Ravioli

Ravioli are perhaps the best-known type of stuffed pasta. They can be either square or rectangular in shape and are common in many parts of Italy. The name *raviolo* is an ancient word for describing pasta that is *riavvolta* (wrapped round) a filling. Ravioli are served with a variety of sauces: mushroom, tomato, meat and many others.

To prepare ravioli: roll out the egg pasta dough and place little mounds of stuffing about 4 cm ($1\frac{1}{2}$ in) apart in a row about 4 cm ($1\frac{1}{2}$ in) from the edge of the sheet of dough. Fold the outside edge of the dough over the mounds of stuffing, then cut off the strip of stuffed pasta with the pastry wheel and press the dough down round the filling to seal it tightly. Finally, use the pastry wheel to divide the strip into fairly large rectangles of filled pasta. If you are making ravioli for soup, make smaller ones.

Cannelloni with Mascherpone

40

Rotolo

This is a type of large cannellone or roll made from egg pasta dough and generally filled with a mixture of spinach or chard and ricotta.

To prepare rotolo: roll out the egg pasta dough into a long, wide rectangle and spread the stuffing over the dough. Roll it up on itself keeping the roll nice and tight and closing the ends as if it were a packet. Wrap it in muslin, tie it in several places and poach it in a large quantity of simmering salted water.

Cut into slices about 1 cm ($\frac{1}{2}$ in) thick and served with the sauce of your choice (see recipe page 168), rotolo makes a substantial and tasty main dish.

Tortelli with Tails

This variety of stuffed pasta has the distinctive shape of a twisted sweet and is usually filled with spinach, ricotta, mascherpone cheese, Parmesan cheese and eggs. It is served with melted butter, sage and Parmesan or with tomato sauce.

To prepare tortelli with tails: make the ordinary egg pasta dough and roll it out as thinly as possible. Place little mounds of filling 7.5 to 10 cm (3 to 4 in) apart in a row about 4 cm ($1\frac{1}{2}$ in) from the edge of the sheet of dough. Then fold the dough over the filling to enclose it. Cut off the filled strip in the usual way and press the pasta down around the filling. Divide the strip into long rectangles. Take the ends of each rectangle and begin to twist them gently. Continue as if wrapping sweets.

Tortellini or Cappelletti

These are an Emilian speciality, from Bologna to be precise. Tortellini are nearly always served in broth, but can be accompanied by tomato or Bolognese sauce. They are sometimes served in vol-au-vents, with a cream sauce.

To prepare tortellini: roll out the egg pasta dough as usual; take small quantities of stuffing and place them 2 to 3 cm ($\frac{3}{4}$ to $1\frac{1}{4}$ in) apart in a row about 3 cm ($1\frac{1}{4}$ in) from the edge of the sheet of dough. Then fold over the outside edge of the dough to cover the little mounds of stuffing. Cut off the strip of stuffed pasta with the pastry wheel, and press the dough down around each mound of filling to hold it in. Still

Different types of home-made pasta and stuffed pasta

using the pastry wheel, cut the strip of stuffed pasta into little rectangles. To finish, overlap the two bottom corners of the rectangle to give the tortellini the shape of a little hat.

REGIONAL VARIETIES OF PASTA

This section deals with some regional varieties of pasta which are prepared in much the same way as home-made egg pasta. Originating in different regions of Italy, these types of pasta have become well known and are now part of the national gastronomic heritage.

The dough is made by hand and the shapes are formed with the help of presses and other basic utensils.

The flour used is either hard wheat or hard wheat flour mixed with ordinary white flour, wholewheat flour, buckwheat flour or white flour mixed with bran. For certain types of pasta, breadcrumbs, chestnut flour, vegetables or eggs are added to the flour.

Bigoli

Bigoli are a typically Venetian dish resembling thick spaghetti. They are made from hard wheat flour or with half hard wheat flour and half ordinary white flour (white bigoli), or with wholewheat flour (dark bigoli) mixed with water. Nowadays bigoli are enriched with other ingredients which make the dough softer and tastier. Bigoli can be made by mixing 350 g (12 oz) of either strong flour or wholewheat flour with 3 eggs, salt, about 30 g (1 oz) butter and enough milk to make a fairly consistent dough. The dough is put through the *bigolaro,* a manually operated press, and the long spaghetti-like pasta, cut into lengths of about 30 cm (12 in) as it comes out of the machine, is collected in a wide floured receptacle or basket.

Bigoli are served with various sauces, such as duck sauce, onion and anchovy sauce, fresh sardines sautéed in oil and garlic or chicken giblet sauce.

Different types of regional pasta (here, clockwise from left, panciuti, trofie, ceriole, orecchiette, malloreddus)

Corzetti

Corzetti are a type of pasta from Liguria, so-called because their shape is similar to that of the *crosazzo,* the ancient silver coin of the seafaring Republic of Genoa. They are made from white flour, eggs, salt and warm water in sufficient quantities to obtain a consistent dough. Sometimes boiled spinach is added.

In Liguria the corzetti are made as follows: the dough is rolled out in a fairly thick sheet and little discs are cut out with the appropriate stamp (a *crosetti* iron) which leaves an Arabic-style pattern impressed on the discs. To form corzetti at home you can break off little pieces of dough about the size of chick-peas, stretch and pinch the pieces to form a shape like a full figure of 8.

Corzetti are served with alternating layers of melted butter and finely chopped sweet marjoram with a good pinch of freshly milled black pepper, or with a Bolognese or mushroom sauce.

Garganelli

A speciality from Romagna, these are fluted maccheroni made from a mixture of white flour and grated Parmesan cheese, eggs, nutmeg, and salt. For 400 g (14 oz) flour allow 4 tablespoons of grated cheese and 4 eggs. You need a special utensil called a *pettine* (comb) which is a wooden block (made of cane) with ridges on the upper surface, and a thin stick.

Mix the flour, cheese, eggs, a few pinches of nutmeg and salt into a dough, then, flouring the pastry board from time to time, roll out the dough. Keep the bulk of the dough covered with a cloth and cut a little of the dough at a time into 3.5 cm ($1\frac{1}{3}$ in) squares. Then wrap one corner of a square of dough round the thin rod; continue to roll it round the rod pressing it over the *pettine*. The ridges on the *pettine* give the maccheroni a fluted appearance similar to fluted penne. Remove the garganello from the rod and continue likewise with the other squares of dough. If you do not have the appropriate utensils, you can use a ridged wooden board (the same as for potato gnocchi) and a round pencil. You can also work directly on the pastry board but the maccheroni will come out smooth.

Garganelli are usually served with a bacon sauce.

Garganelli with Bacon Sauce

Hollow Maccheroni or Maccaruni

Hollow maccheroni or *maccheroni inferrettati* are very common all over southern Italy as well as in Sicily and Sardinia. As the name denotes, these are a type of long maccheroni with a hole in the centre. They are sometimes called fusilli. They are made with white flour and hard wheat flour mixed with water and salt.

To make them: mix 300g (10oz) white flour and 150g (5oz) strong flour with sufficient slightly salted water to make a firm dough. A special square-sectioned iron needle can be used, or a large knitting needle, or even a stick of willow, which is more supple and easier to manage. Cut the dough into pieces and cover with a cloth to stop them drying out. Then roll a piece of dough into a cylindrical shape about as thick as a pencil, and cut into lengths of between 6 to 20cm ($2\frac{1}{2}$ to 8in) depending on how long you want the maccheroni to be. Lay 2 or 3 pieces close to each other on the pastry board. Put the needle up against the centre of the rolls of dough. Pressing on the needle and on the dough push the needle into the dough, moving it backwards and forwards to hollow out the centre. Remove the maccheroni from the needle and allow them to dry on the pastry board.

Maccheroni can be served in a variety of ways: with tomato and oregano sauce, tomato, olive and caper sauce, with garlic, oil and sweet peppers or with tomato and aubergine sauce.

Malloreddus

A Sardinian speciality, malloreddus are a type of tiny, fluted gnocchi (dumplings) made from hard wheat flour, water and salt. A pinch of saffron may also be added. The shapes are made with an instrument called a *ciurili,* a kind of sieve woven of very fine rushes or twisted string.

To make malloreddus: mix strong flour, salt and water to a firm but not too hard homogenous dough. Break off a small piece and roll it with your hands to obtain a longish roll about $\frac{1}{2}$cm ($\frac{1}{4}$in) wide. Then break off little pieces about the size of a bean and rub them on the rush threads to obtain the distinctive texture and sea-shell shape.

Before cooking, allow to dry for 24 hours. Serve with a sauce made from lamb, kid or game, tomatoes and bacon.

Malloreddus are also made commercially from hard wheat flour.

Orecchiette

This is a typical pasta from Apulia in southern Italy. It is also known as *strascicati* or *strascinati* (dragged pasta) because it is made by pressing or dragging the dough on a rough wooden table. Orecchiette are shaped like tiny 'ears' (hence their name in Italian), shells or hats and are made from hard wheat flour and white flour mixed with water and salt. To make orecchiette: mix 350 g (12 oz) white flour, 100 g (3½ oz) strong flour and enough warm water to make a fairly firm dough, a little stiffer than that used to make bread.

Break off a piece of dough and roll it out on the floured pastry board until it is cylindrical and about the thickness of a pencil. Then cut it into lengths of 1 cm (½ in). Using a rounded knife like a palette knife, press each piece over the pastry board. The dough will roll up into a shell shape. You can also shape them on the tip of the thumb.

Cook with potatoes or broccoli and season with tomato sauce and pecorino cheese. Orecchiette are also made commercially.

Pizzoccheri

Pizzoccheri come from the mountainous Valtelline area of Lombardy. They are short fat tagliatelle made with buckwheat flour and water, nowadays, in the proportions of 300 g (10 oz) buckwheat flour to 100 g (3½ oz) white flour, with 1 egg, salt and a little milk to form a homogenous, fairly firm dough. The dough is rolled out into a not too thin sheet and cut into strips about 1 cm (½ in) wide. The strips are then cut into segments 5 to 6 cm (2 to 2½ in) long.

The noodles are cooked in water with the varieties of vegetables eaten in the mountains, such as potatoes and Savoy cabbage, and seasoned with layers of melted butter, sage and whole cloves of garlic alternating with slices of Bitto cheese (you can substitute fontina). Given the substantial accompaniments (vegetables, cheese and butter), the dish becomes a meal in itself. You can buy commercially produced pizzoccheri in the shops, but they taste nothing like the home-made variety.

Stringozzi or Ceriole

Ceriole is a typical dish from Umbria. They are a type of long maccheroni with holes in the centre and are made from hard wheat flour mixed with salted water in sufficient quantities to obtain a fairly consistent dough. Use the special square-sectioned iron needle if possible, but a large knitting needle may be substituted.

To make ceriole at home: knead the dough energetically for some time, beating it repeatedly on the pastry board. Roll it into a thick sheet and cut into long wide strips. Flour your hands and roll the iron needle across the strips of dough so that they curl round it. Let them dry a little before removing them.

Ceriole are served with a spicy tomato, garlic and oil sauce, or baked with garlic and oil.

Strozzapreti or Strangolapreti

Strozzapreti is a typical dish from Lucca in Tuscany. They are a thin type of bucatini, about 6 cm ($2\frac{1}{2}$ in) long and made from white flour and hot water. To make them: mix the flour and water with a wooden spoon until a dough of the right consistency is obtained – neither too hard nor too soft. To obtain a richer dough, add eggs and use less hot water. Then knead the dough by hand on the pastry board for about 15 minutes and shape it into long sticks about the thickness of your little finger. Cut into pieces about 2.5 cm (1 in) long. Roll the pieces round a knitting needle to obtain short bucatini with a hole in the centre. Leave to dry.

Strozzapreti are served with a meat sauce, pecorino cheese and black pepper.

Trofie

Trofie are a Ligurian speciality. They are small gnocchi (dumplings) with twisted tapering ends, generally made from white flour and bran. The ratio is 350 g (12 oz) white flour to 60 g (2 oz) bran mixed with enough slightly salty water to make a firm dough. Sometimes chestnut flour is added in tiny amounts to sweeten the gnocchi and blend with the sauce.

To make trofie, cut the dough into pieces, roll each piece on the floured pastry board to obtain a thin stick shape, then cut off pieces about the size of a chick-pea or a little larger. With your right thumb roll each piece on the pastry board to form a twisted dumpling with tapering ends, measuring about 3 cm ($1\frac{1}{4}$ in) in length.

To save time, you can make the gnocchi bigger and flatten them with a fork as for potato gnocchi. Trofie are boiled on their own or sometimes with fresh white beans. They are often served with pesto sauce (made by crushing fresh basil, garlic, pine nuts, pecorino or Parmesan cheese, salt and lots of olive oil with a pestle in a mortar) or a variant of the sauce containing other ingredients such as walnuts, paprika or chilli powder.

THE MEDITERRANEAN DIET

Proponents of the 'Mediterranean diet' suggest it is the healthiest and most balanced diet there is. Based on pasta as a staple, it is a diet that isn't a diet, a way of eating healthily, spending less, and preserving health by going back to what was once considered the food of the poor (cereals, vegetables and oil).

It is a diet that is advocated by Italy's National Institute of Nutrition, by the health-conscious and by many Italian nutritionists who have now endorsed it from the dietary point of view. It is a diet that is particularly recommended for the prevention and alleviation of cardio-vascular disease because it is low in animal fat and sugar.

The nutritional properties of pasta come from the high starch (carbo-hydrate) content (70-75%), from the relatively high protein content (11-12%), the presence of some vitamins and minerals and a little fibre. The fat content is low (less than 1%). The calorific value of pasta is about 350 calories per 100 g ($3\frac{1}{2}$ oz), the average portion size. Whole-wheat pasta contains additional protein and approximately 10% by weight of dietary fibre. All types of pasta are quickly digested and assimilated by the body to aid combustion and provide heat and energy.

But it is not sufficient simply to eat pasta more often; it is necessary to choose the correct combinations of foods, to select food because of its nutritional content and according to individual needs, to serve less sauce and, above all, to make qualitative as well as quantitative choices. It is precisely along these lines that the recipes for pasta dishes in this book have been created and balanced according to the new recommendations of nutritionists.

ADVICE FROM THE EXPERTS

WHAT MAKES GOOD PASTA?

It is almost impossible to recognize good pasta at first sight, particularly commercially made dried pasta, as it is sold in packets or sealed cellophane bags. One indication of quality is the colour which should be even all over. The pasta should have a pleasant smell and be brittle.

The real proof, however, lies in its resistance to cooking. Pasta which has been cooked for the right length of time but which adheres to the saucepan when drained, looks sticky, disintegrates, or is mushy to eat, is definitely unpleasant. It means that the pasta is of poor quality, made with soft wheat flour or with old hard wheat flour, lacking in gluten. It is the gluten which is the strong point of pasta: if there is a high percentage of gluten, the pasta will not go soggy when cooked, but if there is a low percentage, the starch is released, making the pasta sticky.

When it has been cooked, good pasta should not break or unravel. The water should only be slightly cloudy with excess starch and the pasta should have doubled in volume. Once you have found a good make of dried pasta that survives the cooking test, stick to it.

As for shop-bought fresh pasta, it is as well to know that this type of pasta, which enjoys a certain popularity because it is similar to home-made pasta, costs more than dried pasta but is worth less nutritionally as it contains such a high proportion of water. Its freshness, then, does not always represent an advantage over dried pasta.

WHAT MAKES A GOOD SAUCE?

There are many, many different sauces to accompany both home-made and commercially produced pasta. Each of these sauces is capable of transforming pasta into a tasty and substantial main course. There are cooked and uncooked sauces; those made with or without tomatoes; with or without meat; sauces based on cheese, herbs and spices; vegetable sauces; fish sauces; and subtle white sauces—all obtained from a skilful blending of colours and flavours.

To help you in the 'correct' choice of sauce (and it is ultimately a matter of individual taste and preference), you will find some suggestions on pages 57 to 58.

THE TEN GOLDEN RULES FOR COOKING PASTA

1. Use a large deep saucepan so the pasta has plenty of room.

2. Use 1 litre (1¾ pints) of water for every 100g (3½ oz) of pasta. It is best to use fairly hard water. The saucepan should be about three-quarters full.

3. Use about 10-12g (⅓ oz) of salt to 1 litre (1¾ pints) of water. It is preferable to use whole sea-salt (which is now available in supermarkets) especially when cooking for people who suffer from hypertension or cardiovascular diseases.

4. Add the salt only when the water has reached the boil and wait until the salt has all dissolved and the water has returned to the boil before putting in the pasta.

5. Add the pasta, whether fresh or dried, all at once and stir immediately with a long cooking fork or wooden spoon. For long varieties of pasta, stir frequently during the cooking to prevent the pasta from sticking together. For short varieties, stir occasionally during the cooking. As you stir, lift the pasta away from the base of the pan.

6. To stop certain long or thin types of pasta, such as tagliatelle, pappardelle, spaghetti or trenette sticking together, add a drop of oil to the water.

7. Cook in an uncovered saucepan over a high heat.

8. For commercially made pasta, follow the instructions on the packet concerning cooking time; you could keep a note of any variations you make to suit your own taste. For home-made pasta, follow the instructions in the recipe. But whatever cooking time is specified, it is always advisable to test the pasta by tasting a piece to see if it is *al dente* (still a little firm to the bite) before draining it.

9 As soon as the pasta is done, pour a ladleful of cold water into the saucepan to arrest the cooking at once, then drain.

10 For certain types of pasta that are pre-cooked and then finished in the oven (cannelloni and lasagne, for example), make sure the pasta is even more *al dente* than usual when you pre-cook it, and light the oven well in advance so the pasta does not over-cook at the second stage either.

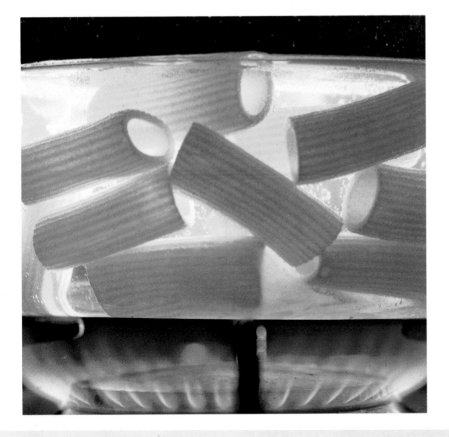

HINTS ON SERVING PASTA

1. Unless you are serving the pasta cold, always warm the tureen or serving dish in the oven or by pouring boiling water into it and drying thoroughly.

2. Immediately after draining the pasta and before mixing it with the sauce, add a spoonful of oil or a knob of butter to prevent it from sticking together.

3. Serve the pasta with some of the sauce and serve the rest very hot in a sauce-boat (otherwise it will sink to the bottom of the serving dish).

4. When serving cheese with the pasta, add the cheese last of all, or serve it separately, when the pasta has completely absorbed the sauce.

5. Do not serve cheese with fish sauces except when specified in certain regional pasta dishes.

6. Grate the cheese just before serving so as to retain all its flavour and aroma.

7. Keep jars of fresh and dried herbs, tubes of anchovy and olive paste and the pepper-mill within reach; they will be useful for whipping up tasty, first-course pasta dishes.

8. If you want to serve pasta that is a brighter yellow, add a pinch of saffron to the cooking water when it begins to boil.

9. Keep back a little of the water the pasta was cooked in if you are serving it with a sauce made with milk, cream or melted cheese. It will make the pasta softer and smoother.

10. Leftover boiled pasta can be added to soups and reheated briefly. If you have a large quantity of leftover pasta you can freeze it.

SAUCES FOR DIFFERENT TYPES OF PASTA

For tagliatelle, fettuccine, lagane, laganelle, lasagnette, linguine, trenette, spaghetti (or any other type of long pasta):
—Hot or cold sauces based on fresh or tinned tomatoes, vegetables and herbs.
—Quick-to-prepare, piquant sauces made with olive oil, garlic, chilli pepper, anchovies.
—Fish sauces, mainly shellfish-based.
—White sauces, made from cream, mascherpone cheese or soft cheeses that melt easily, and often containing curry powder, saffron, nutmeg or other spices.

For fusilli, zite, zitoni, torciglioni, viti, bucatini (or other types of dried twisted or hollow pasta):
—Vegetable sauces based on green vegetables cooked in a fresh or tinned tomato sauce, and such vegetables as sweet peppers, aubergines, courgettes, olives and capers.

For fine spaghetti, capelli d'angelo, egg tagliatelle, vermicelli (or any type of very thin long pasta):
—Uncooked butter and cheese.
—Melted butter with sage and cheese.
—Sauces made with egg.
—Raw fresh tomato sauces.

For pappardelle, and home-made or commercial tagliatelle:
—Ragù made with minced beef or pork.
—Ragù containing sausage.
—Ragù containing giblets.
—Vegetable sauces, especially mushroom and artichoke.
—Stews.

For short ditalini, little penne, gobbetti, mezze maniche, sedanini, avemarie (or other very short varieties of pasta served with a sauce):
—Vegetable sauces, always with a tomato base, and particularly those containing pulses such as beans, lentils and chick-peas.

For lasagne, both home-made and commercially produced:
—Ragù made with minced beef or pork.
—Ragù containing sausage.
—Ragù containing mushrooms.
—Fresh or dried mushroom sauces.
—Ragùs or tomato sauces that have been enriched with béchamel.

For Regional and Fresh Pasta

Each type requires a particular sauce, depending on local tradition.

Orecchiette: *(little ear or shell-shapes from Apulia)*
—tomato sauce and boiled potatoes
—tomato sauce flavoured with garlic, with broccoli or grated turnips
—tomato sauce with veal rolls

Malloreddus: *(small Sardinian gnocchi)*
—tomato and bacon sauce with basil
—lamb or sausage ragù

Cavatieddi: *(small shell shapes from Apulia)*
—meat sauce
—fresh tomato sauce flavoured with basil
—garlic, oil and chilli sauce

Pizzoccheri: *(small lasagne from the Valtelline)*
—melted butter flavoured with garlic and sage alternated with Bitto
  cheese, potatoes and boiled cabbage

Maccheroni alla chitarra: *(long spaghetti from the Abruzzi)*
—lamb ragù
—tomato sauce with olives, capers and anchovies
—tomato sauce with sweet peppers, aubergines and chilli pepper
—raw tomato mixed with lots of olive oil and some oregano

Bigoli: *(a type of Venetian spaghetti)*
—fish sauces based on fresh sardines, flavoured with garlic
—giblet sauce
—onion and anchovy sauce
—duck sauce
—tomato, sweet pepper and olive sauce

CAN PASTA BE FROZEN?

It most certainly can, provided you follow certain tips to ensure that the pasta is frozen perfectly and will taste like a dish of freshly made pasta.

You can freeze both cooked and uncooked pasta. But what are the advantages? They are numerous. In the first place, it saves time and energy. To make a batch of tagliatelle, for example, that will serve eight people rather than four takes only a tiny bit longer. So, next time you are making a quantity for four, double the ingredients and you will be able to freeze half the pasta for use in an emergency when guests turn up unexpectedly.

How to Freeze Fresh Uncooked Pasta

After cutting the dough into the various shapes, let them dry for a while by spreading them out on the pastry board. Then divide (or weigh) the shapes into individual portions and package them for freezing. You can either use polythene bags or well-sealed plastic containers. The pasta will keep for several months, depending on the star markings of your freezer or refrigerator freezing compartment. When you use the pasta, cook it immediately without thawing.

You can also freeze uncooked filled varieties of pasta, such as ravioli, tortellini, agnolini and others, for several months. Before freezing filled pasta, spread the pieces on a tray and put them in the freezer for about an hour. This will make the pieces go very hard and prevent them from sticking together once they are inside the freezer bag. Put the pieces in airtight polythene bags (which can be bought anywhere, especially in supermarkets) dividing the pasta into portions to suit the requirements of your household (or individual portions so that you always thaw only the amount needed). Then label each bag with a self-adhesive label stating the contents, the date of freezing and the maximum length of time it can be frozen.

When you want to use frozen filled pasta, do not thaw it first but put it straight into boiling water or stock, depending on whether you intend to eat it drained with a sauce or in a soup.

How to Freeze Cooked Pasta

The best type of cooked pasta to freeze is the dried, commercially produced pasta made from durum wheat flour, because it 'resists' cooking better and does not break. It is advisable to choose the larger varieties which do not become over-cooked and stand up better to being heated in the oven *au gratin*.

With egg pasta too the best types for freezing (with a few exceptions) are the dried, commercially produced ones, made with 4 eggs to 1 kg ($2\frac{1}{4}$ lb) of flour, rather than home-made pasta, because they stand up to cooking better. To freeze cooked pasta, it is important to follow certain essential rules:

—Use best-quality olive oil to season the pasta and in small amounts as the oil content tends to reduce the length of time the pasta can be preserved. It is always possible to add oil once the pasta has been thawed.

—Use salt sparingly when boiling the pasta to begin with and when preparing the sauce: salt tends to dehydrate food.

—Add spices and herbs in small amounts because their flavour may intensify with freezing and subsequent reheating. You can always add more later.

—It is advisable to avoid using cream and egg yolk in the accompanying sauce: they can be added at the last minute.

—You can use frozen raw vegetables in the preparation of vegetable sauces. They can be refrozen after being cooked.

—Ensure that all frozen dishes have a label indicating the content, number of portions, date of cooking and the expiry date.

—Keep the containers that have been in the freezer longest at the front so as not to keep them longer than the expiry date.

And here is what you do:

For plain pasta The pasta should be cooked *al dente* and drained. Freeze in polythene bags or plastic containers (as with fresh pasta). It is sometimes useful to freeze leftover plain pasta or to cook it and freeze it in preparation for a large party but on the whole plain pasta takes little time to cook and will have a better consistency if it is not cooked twice.

Freezing pasta dishes

For integral pasta dishes like spaghetti Bolognese The pasta should be cooked *al dente*—or even slightly firmer than usual. Arrest the cooking by adding a little cold water to the saucepan, drain the pasta and add the prepared sauce. Allow to cool by standing the dish in a large bowl of cold water (making sure that the water level is not higher than that of the dish). Then pour the pasta into the container to go in the freezer—use a container made of plastic, glass, earthenware or Pyrex. You can buy special freezer containers made from thick tin foil with airtight, waxed cardboard covers. Bolognese sauce can also be frozen separately.

For filled cannelloni You can use either home-made or commercial pasta. After cooking the pasta *al dente,* drain, leave to dry and fill with the prepared stuffing. Roll up the cannelloni and lay them in the containers, alternating the sauce and the cheese. If you are using earthenware dishes or containers without lids, cover with clingfilm or aluminium foil, making the container as airtight as possible. Finally, label the containers with the contents and dates as suggested above and place in the freezer. If you use tin foil containers (or ovenproof dishes) you can remove the lids and put the containers directly in the oven when you want to reheat the cannelloni.

For lasagne Proceed as for cannelloni.

For rotoli with non-meat fillings After rolling out the home-made egg pasta into a rectangle (as explained in the recipe on p. 168), put in the filling then roll it up in a sausage shape and wrap a fine white cloth or piece of muslin round it to bind it. Put the roll in a polythene bag and freeze. Remove from the freezer several hours in advance and allow to thaw partially, then immerse the roll (still wrapped in the cloth) in a large pan of lightly salted boiling water and boil for 40 minutes to 1 hour (depending on how much the roll has thawed) over a moderate heat to prevent the roll from breaking. Slice while it is hot, and serve with melted butter, sage and Parmesan cheese or with a cream and mushroom sauce.

How Long Can Dishes Be Kept in the Freezer?

That depends on the ingredients: the heavier the sauce and the more oil it contains, the shorter the time it will keep. As a guideline, a pasta dish can be kept in the freezer for up to three months. After that, it will gradually begin to lose some of its quality, consistency, flavour and aroma. This recommendation is for a freezer at a temperature of between $-25°$ to $-30°C$ ($-13°$ to $-22°F$). Pasta can be kept for up to six months at a lower temperature still.

How to Thaw and Reheat Pasta

There are several methods: some are appropriate for pasta on its own and others for integral pasta dishes or for dishes that are cooked in the oven with fillings. Plain pasta should be thawed in the refrigerator until it comes free from the sides of the container. Then plunge it into boiling water. When the water returns to the boil the pasta is heated through.

Integral pasta dishes, such as spaghetti with Bolognese sauce, are thawed by keeping the still-sealed container at room temperature for a few hours. The pasta is then transferred to a *bain-marie* or double-boiler and heated over simmering water. When the pasta is sufficiently hot, you can add the final seasonings of herbs, cheese, salt and pepper.

Alternatively, as soon as you take the container out of the freezer, you can immerse it in a pan half-filled with boiling water (off the heat), and when the pasta has come free from the sides of the container, transfer it to a *bain-marie* or double-boiler to reheat it.

A third method is to take the container out of the freezer and put it in the bottom of the refrigerator for twenty-four hours. The next day, transfer the contents to a *bain-marie* or double-boiler and reheat gently.

Lasagne and other types of filled pasta should be thawed in the bottom of the refrigerator or at room temperature. Then, after removing the lid, place in the centre of the oven at $180°$-$200°C$ ($350°$-$400°F$, mark 4-6). After about a quarter of an hour, cover the top with aluminium foil to stop the surface burning before the lasagne is heated through. Remove the foil 5 minutes before serving. Add a few knobs of butter or a few spoonfuls of cream and a little cheese too, if you wish.

You can also put lasagne, and any of the other types of filled pasta, straight from the freezer into the oven. If you do this, keep the oven low at $150°C$ ($300°F$, mark 2) for at least 30 minutes to thaw the pasta (you can test if it is thawed by plunging a fork into the centre). Turn the oven up to $200°C$ ($400°F$, mark 6) to heat the dish through and obtain a perfect gratin.

PASTA WITH RAGÙ
(MEAT SAUCES)

A ragù is a meat sauce made in the same way as a meat stew. Bolognese sauce is the best-known example but there are many variations. Ragù can be made from minced beef, veal or pork, giblets or a combination of various red and white meats, which are simmered gently with a mixture of sautéed chopped vegetables (onions, carrots, celery, garlic), flavoured with aromatic herbs (parsley, basil, sage, rosemary, bay leaves) and moistened with a liquid such as stock or wine. At one time, especially in central and southern Italy, ragù was made, not from minced meat, but from a large piece of beef that was cooked very slowly until it disintegrated and blended in with the sauce. Nowadays, minced meat is used to save time and money.

The recommended cuts of meat are economical rather than prime cuts, or those that are part lean and part fat, like blade and shoulder, brisket and thin rib of beef. Sometimes, sausage, ham or bacon is used alone or added to minced meat to improve the flavour and texture of the ragù.

There are two types of ragù: 'red' ragù, which is made with tomatoes, and 'white' ragù, which does not include tomatoes. There are also many regional variations. Tasty, piquant sauces are made from game cooked with a mixture of chopped vegetables and ham, or from lamb and kid with herbs and spices. The meats are simmered slowly while, during the cooking, various liquids are added depending on the locality: dry white wine, red wine, fortified wines such as Marsala, Madeira or Vin Santo, or some good (preferably home-made) stock.

Ragù should be prepared in quantity, some used to season the pasta and the rest served in a sauce-boat with it.

The recipes that follow will serve 6 as a first course or 4 as a main course.

Some ingredients for ragù, and commercial dried pasta (here, fluted maccheroni and lumaconi)

Fusilli with Sausage and Mushroom Ragù

Time: 45 minutes
Ingredients
450 g (1 lb) fusilli
300 g (10 oz) mushrooms
3 tbsp olive oil
30 g (1 oz) butter
1 onion, finely chopped
1 carrot, finely chopped
1 bay leaf
225 g (8 oz) spicy Italian poaching
  or frying sausages
1 400 g (14 oz) tin of peeled tomatoes
Salt and pepper
A few tbsp stock
A pinch of mixed herbs

Wipe the mushrooms with a damp cloth and slice them. Heat the oil and butter in a large pan and sauté the onion and carrot gently. Add the bay leaf, the sliced sausage and the sliced mushrooms. Sauté gently. Press the tomatoes through a nylon sieve and add them to the other ingredients in the pan. Add salt and pepper to taste and a few spoonfuls of stock; cover the pan and simmer over a low heat until the sauce thickens. Before removing the pan from the heat, stir in the mixed herbs.

Put the fusilli in boiling salted water, and cook until *al dente*. Drain and serve with the ragù.
Hint: Use fresh herbs when available as they have more flavour. Add them at the last minute.

Spaghetti with Bacon

Time: 30 minutes
Ingredients
450 g (1 lb) spaghetti or bucatini
100 g (3½ oz) bacon or smoked ham
4 to 5 tbsp olive oil
1 small onion, finely chopped
1 small chilli pepper
225 g (8 oz) peeled tomatoes
Salt
60 g (2 oz) grated pecorino cheese

Cut the bacon or ham into small pieces. Heat the oil in a large pan and sauté the bacon until cooked. Remove from the pan, drain and set aside. Sauté the onion and chilli in the same oil. Cut the tomatoes into fine strips and add to the pan. Add salt and simmer for a few minutes. Complete the sauce by adding the bacon and simmering a few more minutes.

Meanwhile, cook the spaghetti in a large pan of boiling, salted water. Drain the pasta when it is *al dente* and serve with the sauce and grated cheese.
Hint: The best cheese to use is a pungent mature pecorino but if not available, use grated Parmesan.

Maltagliati with Ragù

Time: 1½ hours
Ingredients
450 g (1 lb) maltagliati (diamond-
  shaped pasta)

Spaghetti with Bacon

66

60 g (2 oz) butter
2 tbsp olive oil
1 small onion, finely chopped
100 g (3½ oz) minced beef or pork
A few fresh basil leaves
450 g (1 lb) ripe tomatoes, peeled,
   seeded and chopped
Salt
60 g (2 oz) grated Parmesan cheese

Prepare the ragù first: heat the butter and oil in a medium-sized pan and sauté the finely chopped onion until soft. Add 2 table-spoons of water. After 5 minutes, add the minced meat and let it absorb the flavours for a few minutes. Add the basil leaves and tomatoes. Add salt to taste and cook the ragù for about 1 hour over a moderate heat, stirring from time to time.

Preheat the oven to 180°C (350°F, mark 4). Cook the mal-tagliati in a large saucepanful of boiling salted water and drain well. Arrange the pasta in layers in an ovenproof dish, spooning a little ragù between each layer. The last layer should be of ragù. Put the dish in the oven for 15 minutes, which is just long enough to brown the top of the pasta. Serve with the grated cheese.

Hint: To make the ragù even tastier, use half minced beef and half minced pork or sausagemeat.

Penne with Pork Ragù

Time: 1 hour
Ingredients
450 g (1 lb) penne
3 to 4 tbsp olive oil
60 g (2 oz) bacon, diced
1 onion, chopped
1 carrot, chopped
1 tbsp chopped basil and parsley
225 g (8 oz) minced pork
Salt and pepper
125 ml (4 fl oz) red wine
1 300 g (10 oz) tin of peeled tomatoes
A few tbsp stock (optional)

Heat 3 to 4 tablespoons of oil in a pan and sauté the diced bacon, then add the chopped onion, carrot and herbs. Leave to cook for a minute or two. Add the minced pork, salt and pepper and, when the meat is browned, pour in the red wine. Simmer until the wine has evaporated, press the tomatoes through a nylon sieve and add to the other ingredients. Cover and cook the ragù on a low heat, stirring from time to time. Add a little boiling water from time to time or, better still, water and a little stock.

Boil the penne in salted water, drain the pasta when it is *al dente* and serve with the ragù.

Hint: Fresh tomatoes may be substituted for the tinned peeled tomatoes.

Maccheroni with Meat Ball Ragù

Time: 1 hour
Ingredients
450 g (1 lb) small fluted maccheroni
The soft crumb of 1 bread roll,
    crust discarded
2 tbsp milk
300 g (10 oz) minced beef
100 g (3½ oz) cooked ham or
    mortadella, chopped
1 tbsp chopped parsley mixed with
    1 crushed clove garlic
60 g (2 oz) grated Parmesan cheese
A pinch of grated nutmeg
1 egg
Salt
1 small onion, chopped
3 to 4 tbsp oil
A small bunch of fresh basil
1 400 g (14 oz) tin of peeled tomatoes
    or 175 ml (6 fl oz) home-made
    tomato sauce

Soften the bread in the milk, then squeeze out the excess milk. Mix the minced beef, the chopped ham, parsley, cheese, nutmeg, egg, bread and salt in a bowl. Make little balls of the mixture, about the size of cherries. Sauté the onion in 3 to 4 tablespoons of hot oil in a saucepan. Add the bunch of basil and the tomatoes. Salt, and simmer until the sauce has reduced. Remove the basil and add the meatballs. Simmer for about 15 minutes, stirring.

Boil the pasta in a large saucepanful of salted water, drain when it is *al dente* and pour part of the sauce over the maccheroni. Transfer the pasta to the middle of a round, fairly deep dish, arrange the meatballs around the outside with a little sauce and serve with the rest of the sauce in a sauceboat.

Hint: Serve as a main course as the meatball sauce makes a fairly substantial meal. As an accompaniment you could serve a mixed raw vegetable salad, depending on the season.

Conchiglie with Würstel

Time: 40 minutes
Ingredients
450 g (1 lb) conchiglie
4 tbsp olive oil
1 small onion, chopped
1 rasher of smoked bacon, diced
225 g (8 oz) German Würstel
    sausages
1 300 g (10 oz) tin of peeled tomatoes
    or 1 small tin of tomato purée
Salt and pepper
A bunch of fresh basil

Heat the oil and sauté the onion, then add the bacon to the onion. Dip the Würstel in boiling water for a few seconds, remove the skin, slice and add to the browned onions and bacon. Press the tomatoes through a nylon sieve, and add to the other ingredients, stirring well. Add salt and pepper, and the basil leaves. Simmer, stirring from time to time until the ragù has thickened.

Cook the conchiglie in boiling water, drain when the pasta is *al dente* and serve with the ragù.

Hint: Serve with grated Parmesan cheese if you wish.

Torciglioni with Sausages

Time: 45 minutes
Ingredients
450 g (1 lb) torciglioni (dried pasta twists)
1 300 g (10 oz) tin of peeled tomatoes or 1 small tin of tomato purée
1 onion, finely chopped
A few fresh sage leaves
Salt and pepper
75 ml (2½ fl oz) stock
2 tbsp olive oil
300 g (10 oz) fresh Italian poaching or frying sausages

Press the tomatoes through a nylon sieve into a saucepan and add the onion, the sage leaves, salt, pepper and a little stock. Simmer. Meanwhile, heat the oil in a frying pan and sauté the sausages for about 15 minutes. Drain off the fat and add the sausages to the tomato sauce which will have reduced and thickened. Simmer for another 15 minutes, adding more stock if necessary.

Boil the torciglioni in a large saucepanful of salted water, drain when the pasta is *al dente,* and place on a serving dish. Pour some of the sauce over the pasta and arrange the sausages around the dish. Then pour over the rest of the simmering sauce.

Hint: A nylon sieve is better than a metal one for puréeing tomatoes as it will not react with the acid in the tomatoes to give a metallic taste.

Garganelli with Bacon Sauce

Time: 1½ hours
Ingredients
450 g (1 lb) garganelli (see page 46) or fusilli
Salt and pepper
3 to 4 tbsp olive oil
150 g (5 oz) smoked bacon, diced
175 ml (6 fl oz) home-made tomato sauce

Spread the garganelli out on a pastry board and when they are dry cook them in a large saucepanful of boiling salted water. Heat the olive oil in a large frying pan and sauté the bacon. Drain the pasta when it is *al dente* and add to the bacon. Then add the well-seasoned home-made tomato sauce, mix well and remove the pan from the heat. Before serving, sprinkle liberally with freshly milled pepper.

Torciglioni with Sausages

Hint: If you do not have the appropriate utensil for making the pasta squares, roll them round a stick on the pastry board. If you wish, you may complete the seasoning with grated pecorino cheese.

Orecchiette with Veal and Pork Rolls

Time: 1¾ hours
Ingredients
450 g (1 lb) fresh or dried orecchiette (see page 49)
300 g (10 oz) very thin veal escalopes
300 g (10 oz) thinly sliced pork loin
Salt and pepper
150 g (5 oz) smoked bacon, chopped
150 g (5 oz) grated Parmesan and pecorino cheeses
A bunch of fresh parsley, chopped
2 to 3 tbsp olive oil
1 small onion, chopped
125 ml (4 fl oz) full-bodied red wine
1 225 g (8 oz) tin of peeled tomatoes or 1 small tin of tomato purée

Spread the slices of veal and pork on the kitchen table, sprinkle with salt and a pinch of pepper and scatter some of the chopped bacon, some flakes of cheese and parsley on top. Roll up the meat into roulades, taking care to keep the stuffing in, and fasten the ends with toothpicks.

Heat 2 to 3 tablespoons of oil in a large pan and sauté the onion. Add the meat roulades and brown all over. Pour in the red wine and allow to evaporate completely. Press the tomatoes through a nylon sieve and add them to the other ingredients in the pan. Simmer until the sauce thickens. A few minutes before removing from the heat, add a little cheese.

Boil the orecchiette in a large saucepanful of lightly salted water, drain when the pasta is *al dente* and place on a serving dish. Pour some of the sauce and the rest of the cheese over the pasta and arrange the little rolls around the edge with the rest of the sauce. Serve at once.

Hint: Orecchiette can also be served *in bianco*, that is, in a sauce made from best-quality extra virgin olive oil, garlic, mashed anchovy fillets and boiled turnip tops.

Italian-Style Orecchiette with Ragù

Time: 1½ hours
Ingredients
450 g (1 lb) fresh or dried orecchiette (see page 49)
10 g (⅓ oz) dried mushrooms
A knob of butter
2 to 3 tbsp olive oil
30 g (1 oz) smoked ham, sliced
30 g (1 oz) bacon, sliced
1 carrot, sliced
1 onion, sliced

Italian-Style Orecchiette with Ragù

1 stick celery, chopped
1 clove garlic, sliced
1 clove
225 g (8 oz) minced beef
100 g (3½ oz) minced veal
Salt and pepper
1 bouquet garni of fresh thyme,
    marjoram and a bay leaf
    (optional)
3 tbsp red wine
10 g (⅓ oz) flour
200 g (7 oz) peeled tomatoes
60 g (2 oz) grated pecorino cheese

Soak the mushrooms in warm water, drain and slice them. Heat the butter and oil in a large pan and sauté the sliced mushrooms, ham, bacon, carrot, onion, celery and garlic for a few minutes. Add the clove, the minced beef and veal and salt and pepper to taste. Stir. As soon as the meat begins to brown, add the bouquet garni and pour in the wine. Cook for 30 minutes. When the sauce has reduced, add the flour to thicken it. Press the tomatoes through a nylon sieve and add to the pan. Simmer for another 30 minutes.

Boil the orecchiette in salted water, drain and serve with the hot ragù and grated pecorino cheese.

Hint: Even without the fresh herbs, which are not always available, the ragù will still be tasty. If you like, you can add more dried mushrooms, which are available from Italian delicatessens.

Tagliatelle with Lamb and Curry Sauce

Time: 1 hour 20 minutes
Ingredients
450 g (1 lb) fresh or dried tagliatelle
A shoulder of lamb weighing about
    1 kg (2¼ lb)
A little olive oil
60 g (2 oz) butter
1 shallot, chopped
A large pinch of curry powder
Salt and pepper
200 ml (7 fl oz) single cream

Rinse and dry the lamb and cut into smallish pieces. Heat the oil with half the butter in a large pan and brown the lamb pieces. Add the chopped shallot, the curry powder, salt and pepper and pour in the cream. Cover the pan and simmer on a very low heat for about 1 hour or until the meat is tender.

Remove the lamb pieces from the sauce, strain the sauce and pour it back into the saucepan. Add the pieces of meat and simmer for a few minutes to reheat.

Boil the tagliatelle in a large saucepanful of salted water. Drain when the pasta is *al dente*. Stir in knobs of butter and some of the sauce. Pour the tagliatelle on to a preheated serving dish and arrange the meat around the edge. Pour the rest of the sauce over.

Hint: Serve as a main course. If you like exotic flavours, increase the quantity of curry powder. You can also add a pinch of saffron if you wish.

Fettuccine with Bolognese Sauce

Time: 1½ hours
Ingredients
450 g (1 lb) fresh or dried fettuccine
30 g (1 oz) dried mushrooms
15 g (½ oz) butter
1 small onion, chopped
½ carrot, chopped
1 stick celery
A bunch of fresh parsley, chopped
1 clove garlic (optional)
30 g (1 oz) bacon, chopped
225 g (8 oz) minced pork
1 tbsp dry white wine
3 tbsp concentrated tomato purée
Salt and pepper
A pinch of sugar (optional)
A pinch of nutmeg
2 chicken livers, chopped
60 g (2 oz) grated Parmesan cheese

Soak the mushrooms in warm water. Heat the butter in a large pan and sauté the chopped onion, carrot, celery, parsley, garlic and bacon for about 10 minutes. Then add the minced meat and brown it. Pour in the wine and, after a few minutes, add the tomato purée mixed with a little warm water. Add salt, pepper, sugar, nutmeg, the drained, coarsely chopped mushrooms and the chicken livers. Add the water drained from the mushrooms, which is full of flavour, to the sauce. Cover the pan and cook over a low heat for about 1 hour, stirring from time to time.

Cook the fettuccine in a large saucepanful of boiling salted water and drain when the pasta is *al dente*. Serve with the hot ragù and grated cheese.

Hint: If you wish, you may add a few tablespoonfuls of single cream to the ragù. You can also use 300 g (10 oz) of fresh tomatoes instead of tomato purée.

Fettuccine with Basil-Flavoured Sauce

Time: 40 minutes
Ingredients
450 g (1 lb) fresh or dried fettuccine
30 g (1 oz) butter
1 tbsp olive oil
30 g (1 oz) onion, chopped
800 g (1¾ lb) very small ripe
    tomatoes, peeled
Salt and freshly milled pepper
A large bunch of fresh basil

Heat the butter and oil in a pan and brown the chopped onions. Press the tomatoes through a nylon sieve and add to the onions, together with salt and pepper. Simmer for half an hour, stirring from time to time.

Boil the fettuccine in a large saucepanful of salted water. Drain when the pasta is *al dente* and

75

pour into a heated dish. Serve with the simmering tomato sauce which will have reduced by this time. Then sprinkle over the coarsely chopped basil leaves.

Hint: Do not add cheese as the combination of cheese and basil would overpower the delicate flavour of the tomatoes.

Fettuccine with Lamb Sauce

Time: 1½ hours
Ingredients
450 g (1 lb) fresh or dried fettuccine
8 lamb cutlets
A few cloves of garlic
A few sprigs of rosemary
4 to 5 tbsp olive oil
Salt and pepper
4 or 5 rashers bacon
125 ml (4 fl oz) dry white wine
450 g (1 lb) tomatoes, peeled,
  chopped or sliced
1 tbsp chopped parsley
20 g (⅔ oz) butter
60 g (2 oz) grated pecorino cheese

Using a sharp knife, make small incisions in the cutlets and insert strips of garlic and sprigs of rosemary. Put a little oil in a large saucepan and place the cutlets inside. Pour a little more oil over the meat, sprinkle with salt and pepper, cover with the bacon and place the pan over a high heat.

When the meat is well browned all over, pour the wine over and simmer until it evaporates. Then add the tomatoes, some parsley and continue cooking over a gentle heat for about 1 hour.

When the cutlets are nearly cooked, boil the fettuccine in a large saucepanful of salted water. Drain the pasta when it is *al dente*, and place in a serving dish. Add a few knobs of butter, some of the sauce from the lamb, and the cheese. Arrange the cutlets on a large serving dish with the fettuccine in the centre. Pour the rest of the hot sauce over both meat and pasta and serve.

Hint: This is a robust dish which can be made with other cuts of lamb, such as shoulder, or chops.

Pappardelle au Gratin

Time: 1½ hours
Ingredients
450 g (1 lb) fresh or dried green
  pappardelle or wide noodles
2 tbsp olive oil
100 g (3½ oz) bacon, chopped
1 small onion, chopped
1 carrot, chopped
1 stick celery, chopped
1 spicy Italian poaching or frying
  sausage, chopped
Salt and pepper
125 ml (4 fl oz) dry white wine
1 250 g (9 oz) tin of peeled tomatoes
40 g (1½ oz) butter
60 g (2 oz) flour
½ litre (18 fl oz) milk, heated
A pinch of nutmeg
60 g (2 oz) grated Parmesan cheese

Fettuccine with Lamb Sauce

Prepare the ragù: heat the oil and sauté the bacon, onion, carrot and celery. Add the sausage, salt and pepper. As soon as the sausage begins to brown, pour in the white wine which will evaporate. Press the tomatoes through a nylon sieve, add to the ragù and continue simmering over a gentle heat, stirring frequently and adding water or stock if necessary.

Prepare the béchamel sauce: melt the butter and stir in the flour. Gradually pour in the milk; add salt and pepper and a little grated nutmeg to flavour. Simmer for 5 minutes, stirring constantly with a wooden spoon.

Preheat the oven to 180°C (350°F, mark 4). Boil the pappardelle in a large saucepanful of salted water and drain when the pasta is *al dente*. Pour into a large dish and cover with the ragù (leaving about 1 tablespoon in the pan), and the cheese, and stir carefully. Spread the remaining ragù over the base of an oven-proof dish and pour in the pasta. Pour the béchamel over the pasta and put the dish in the oven until the surface is golden brown. Remove the dish from the oven and serve directly.

Hint: Rather than using tinned tomatoes, substitute 800 g (1¾ lb) fresh tomatoes with the peel and seeds removed.

Pappardelle with Hare

Time: 2 hours + marinating time for hare
Ingredients
450 g (1 lb) fresh or dried pappardelle or wide noodles
1 hare weighing about 1.2 kg (2½ lb), dressed
½ litre (18 fl oz) full-bodied red wine
4 to 5 tbsp olive oil
1 large onion, sliced
2 sticks celery, chopped
3 carrots, chopped
1 clove garlic
2 juniper berries
A pinch of thyme
2 cloves
1 bay leaf
Black peppercorns
Salt
30 g (1 oz) dried mushrooms or 400 g (14 oz) fresh mushrooms
20 g (⅔ oz) butter
1 rasher bacon
A little flour
2 to 3 tbsp brandy
60 g (2 oz) grated Parmesan cheese

Rinse and cut the hare into small, similar-sized pieces and set aside the liver.

Put the meat in a dish and pour over the wine and a little oil. Add the sliced onion, one chopped stick of celery and a carrot, the clove of garlic, juniper berries, thyme, cloves, bay leaf, a few peppercorns and salt, and leave to marinate for several hours or overnight.

Pappardelle with Hare

Soak the dried mushrooms in water. Heat the butter and a little oil in a large pan and sauté the remaining onion, celery and carrots together with the chopped bacon. Drain and slice the mushrooms and, after a few minutes, add them to the other ingredients. Remove the pieces of hare from the marinade and drain. Flour lightly and arrange them in the pan with the vegetables. Add salt and, when the meat is well browned, pour in a little wine from the marinade together with the marinade vegetables, but remove the garlic.

Bring to the boil, cover and simmer for about 1 hour, on a low heat, adding the rest of the wine if necessary. Ten minutes before removing the hare from the heat, add the liver. When the cooking is completed, remove the pieces of hare, discard the bay leaf and strain the sauce. Discard the vegetables but purée the liver into the sauce. Bring the sauce to the boil again and add the brandy. Then remove the bones from the hare, put the meat back in the sauce and keep hot.

Boil the pappardelle in a large saucepanful of salted water and drain when the noodles are *al dente*. Flavour the pasta with some of the sauce and cheese. Pour the pasta into a large, fairly deep, serving dish and arrange the pieces of hare on and around the pasta.

Hint: Use cep mushrooms if they are in season. If you have the time allow the hare to marinate for two days.

Fusilli Hunter's-Style

Time: 30 minutes
Ingredients
450 g (1 lb) fusilli
60 g (2 oz) dried mushrooms
4 tbsp olive oil
1 small onion, finely chopped
1 stick celery, finely sliced
1 clove garlic, finely chopped
1 slice of bacon, 1 cm ($\frac{1}{2}$ in) thick, diced
Salt and pepper
4 to 6 tbsp dry white wine
60 g (2 oz) smoked ham, diced
1 bay leaf

Soak the mushrooms in warm water. Heat the oil in a pan and sauté the onion, celery and garlic. As soon as they have browned, add the bacon, salt and pepper. Pour in the wine and when it has evaporated, add the drained mushrooms, ham and bay leaf and simmer for 15 minutes.

Boil the fusilli in a large saucepanful of salted water, drain when the pasta is *al dente* and remove the bay leaf from the sauce before pouring it over the fusilli.

80

Hint: To complete this rich Mediterranean meal, serve a salad of raw vegetables with a *pinzimonio*—an olive oil, pepper and salt dressing, and toasted wholemeal bread.

Tasty Maltagliati Pie

Time: 1 hour
Ingredients
450 g (1 lb) maltagliati (diamond-shaped pasta)
2 tbsp olive oil
60 g (2 oz) butter
1 small onion, chopped
1 carrot, chopped
1 stick celery, chopped
100 g (3½ oz) minced beef
60 g (2 oz) mortadella, chopped
60 g (2 oz) ham, chopped
100 g (3½ oz) fresh sausage, chopped
Salt
2 to 3 tbsp dry white wine
450 g (1 lb) ripe tomatoes or 1 250 g (9 oz) tin of peeled tomatoes
30 g (1 oz) flour
250 ml (9 fl oz) milk, heated
60 g (2 oz) grated Parmesan cheese

In a large saucepan heat the oil and 30 g (1 oz) of the butter and soften the onion, carrot and celery. Add the minced meat, the mortadella, ham and sausage. Brown thoroughly, add salt and sprinkle with the wine. Peel the tomatoes and rub them through a nylon sieve. When the wine has evaporated, add the tomatoes and continue simmering gently.

Melt the remaining butter in a saucepan and add the flour. Stir to remove any lumps and dilute with the milk, poured in a little at a time. Add salt and simmer for 5 minutes.

Boil the maltagliati in a large saucepanful of salted water.

Preheat the oven to 200°C (400°F, mark 6).

Drain the pasta when it is *al dente* and pour the tomato sauce over it, keeping back 2 or 3 tablespoons. Add half the cheese. Pour into an ovenproof dish and cover with the béchamel sauce. Sprinkle the remaining tomato sauce on top and the rest of the Parmesan. Bake in the oven until the cheese has melted and the top is well browned.

Hint: Always preheat the oven to the required temperature before baking a dish. Most ovens take 15 to 20 minutes to reach a specific temperature.

Tagliatelle with Veal Kebabs

Time: 45 minutes
Ingredients
450 g (1 lb) fresh or dried tagliatelle
450 g (1 lb) veal (best end of neck or loin)
500 g (1 lb 2 oz) baby tomatoes
A few sprigs of fresh sage
1 lemon
3 tbsp olive oil

81

Salt and pepper
60 g (2 oz) butter

Preheat the grill to moderately hot.

Cut the meat into large cubes and thread on skewers, with a tomato and a sage leaf between each piece of meat.

Squeeze the lemon and mix the juice with the olive oil, salt and pepper in a bowl.

Place the skewers on a tray and use a pastry brush to baste them with the oil and lemon mixture. Grill, basting and turning the skewers often.

Boil the tagliatelle in a large saucepanful of salted water and drain when the pasta is *al dente*. Mix in knobs of butter and lots of freshly ground pepper. Arrange the skewers on top, pour the juices over the pasta and serve at once.

Hint: This makes an ideal main course as it contains pasta, meat and vegetables.

Tasty Lasagne

Time: 1½ hours
Ingredients
450 g (1 lb) home-made or packet
   lasagne
500 g (1 lb 2 oz) spinach, washed
300 g (10 oz) ricotta
A small bunch of fresh parsley
75 g (2½ oz) grated Parmesan cheese
1 egg

Salt and pepper
A pinch of nutmeg
60 g (2 oz) butter
2 tbsp olive oil
1 small onion, chopped
1 small carrot, chopped
1 stick celery, chopped
A bunch of fresh basil
100 g (3½ oz) minced beef
100 g (3½ oz) spicy Italian poaching
   or frying sausage, chopped
500 g (1 lb 2 oz) ripe tomatoes or
   1 250 g (9 oz) tin of peeled
   tomatoes

Boil the spinach, drain and cut into strips. Rub the ricotta through a sieve and combine with the spinach. Add the chopped parsley, half the Parmesan and the egg, and season with salt, pepper and a pinch of nutmeg. Mix well to obtain a smooth paste.

Heat the butter and oil in a saucepan and sauté the onion, carrot, celery and basil, reserving a small knob of butter for later. Add the meat and the sausage and brown them. Rub the tomatoes through a nylon sieve and add them to the other ingredients in the pan. Season with salt and pepper and simmer for 40 minutes.

Preheat the oven to 200°C (400°F, mark 6).

Boil the lasagne, a few pieces at a time, in a large saucepanful of salted water, drain when the pasta is *al dente* and spread on a clean cloth. Place a layer of lasagne in a buttered ovenproof dish, put a layer of the spinach and ricotta paste on top, cover with lasagne, and sprinkle with the ragù and cheese. Continue alternating layers until the ingredients are used up. Bake for 15-20 minutes.

Hint: Remember to cook dried lasagne a few minutes longer than fresh.

Two-Filling Lasagne Pie

Time: 1 hour 20 minutes
Ingredients
450 g (1 lb) home-made or packet lasagne
30 g (1 oz) dried mushrooms
3 tbsp olive oil
60 g (2 oz) lean bacon, chopped
1 small onion, chopped
200 g (7 oz) lean minced beef
Salt and pepper
2 chicken livers
1 tbsp concentrated tomato purée
1 tbsp flour
600 g (1¼ lb) spinach, washed
100 g (3½ oz) ham, chopped
A pinch of nutmeg
60 g (2 oz) grated Parmesan cheese
1 egg
20 g (¾ oz) butter

Soak the mushrooms in warm water. Heat the oil and sauté the bacon and onion; after a few minutes add the minced beef, salt and pepper, and brown the meat. Remove the gall bladder from the chicken livers, rinse and chop them and add to the other ingredients. Drain the mushrooms thoroughly and chop coarsely before adding them to the rest. Dilute the tomato purée with a little water and pour into the sauce; simmer over a very low heat for about 45 minutes. When the mixture is almost ready, mix the flour with a little water and stir in.

Meanwhile, boil and chop the spinach and mix with the ham. Add the nutmeg, half the cheese, the egg and a pinch of salt. Mix to bind the ingredients.

Preheat the oven to 190°C (375°F, mark 5).

Boil the lasagne, a few pieces at a time, in salted water, drain and dry on a cloth. Butter an ovenproof dish and place a layer of lasagne on the bottom. Then make a layer of ragù sprinkled with Parmesan cheese, another layer of lasagne and then a layer of spinach filling. Continue alternating the layers until you have used up the ingredients, finishing with ragù and cheese. Put the dish in the oven and bake until there is a golden crust on the surface.

Hint: This should be served as a main course as it is very substantial. As an hors-d'oeuvre or accompaniment, serve a mixed green salad with salt, pepper and an olive oil dressing.

Green Lasagne with Bolognese Sauce

Time: 1½ hours
Ingredients
450 g (1 lb) home-made or packet
  lasagne
30 g (1 oz) dried mushrooms
1 small onion, chopped
75 g (1½ oz) butter
2 tbsp olive oil
225 g (8 oz) minced beef
1 250 g (9 oz) tin of peeled tomatoes
Salt and pepper
60 g (2 oz) flour
½ litre (18 fl oz) milk
A pinch of nutmeg
100 g (3½ oz) grated Parmesan
  cheese

If you are making the lasagne yourself, cut the dough to make either round or oblong shapes depending on the shape of the dish you will be using.

Prepare the sauce: soak the mushrooms in warm water. Finely chop the onion and sauté in 20 g (⅔ oz) butter and the oil. Add the mince and brown. Drain and chop the mushrooms and add them to the pan. Simmer for 5 minutes before adding the tomatoes, salt and pepper. Simmer for a further 45 minutes.

Meanwhile, prepare the béchamel sauce: melt the remaining butter and stir in the flour. Heat the milk and stir it in, a little at a time. Add salt and heat the sauce for a few minutes, stirring continuously. Remove from the heat and flavour with nutmeg.

Boil the lasagne, a few pieces at a time, in a large saucepanful of salted water. Drain and lay the pieces out to dry on a clean tea-towel.

Preheat the oven to 190°C (375°F, mark 5).

Cover the bottom of an oven-proof dish with a little ragù and place a round of lasagne (or a layer of rectangles) over it. Then make another layer of ragù, béchamel sauce and cheese. Continue alternating layers until you have used up the ingredients. The last layer should be ragù. Bake in the oven for 15-20 minutes.

Hint: You can prepare the same dish with either yellow or green commercial egg pasta.

Lasagne with Meat Balls

Time: 1¼ hours
Ingredients
350 g (12 oz) home-made or packet
  lasagne
3 eggs
1 soft bread roll
A little milk
350 g (12 oz) lean minced beef
1 tbsp chopped parsley
60 g (2 oz) grated Parmesan cheese
Salt and pepper
2 tbsp flour
A knob of butter
3 tbsp olive oil

1 small onion, chopped
1 stick celery, chopped
1 small carrot, chopped
1 300 g (10 oz) tin of peeled tomatoes
150 ml (5 fl oz) single cream
1 mozzarella cheese
150 g (5 oz) ricotta

Hard boil two of the eggs. Soak the bread in milk to soften it and mix with the minced beef, parsley, the remaining egg, about half the grated cheese, salt and pepper. Make meatballs about the size of walnuts from this mixture and flour them. Cook them gently in the butter in a frying pan.

Heat the oil and sauté the onion, celery and carrot. Rub the tomatoes through a nylon sieve and add to the other vegetables. Add salt and pepper and simmer until the sauce thickens. Remove from the heat and add the cream.

Dice the mozzarella, crush the ricotta with a fork and slice the hard-boiled eggs.

Boil the lasagne, drain it when it is *al dente* and dry on a tea-towel.

Preheat the oven to 190°C (375°F, mark 5).

Pour a few tablespoons of the tomato sauce into an ovenproof dish and place a layer of lasagne on the bottom, then a layer of meatballs. Cover with a layer of mozzarella, ricotta and then another layer of tomato sauce. Continue alternating layers until you have used up the ingredients. Sprinkle the remaining grated cheese on top and bake for about 20 minutes.

Hint: To offset the acidity of the tomatoes, add $\frac{1}{2}$ teaspoon sugar to the sauce. You can also add garlic to the meatball mixture if you wish.

PASTA WITH VEGETABLE SAUCES

Unlike ragù sauces which are based on meat, the sauces in this section are made from fresh vegetables and herbs. The basic ingredient is nearly always tomatoes. The best varieties to use are the little firm round tomatoes with few seeds. Other types may be substituted provided they are ripe (though not over-ripe) and sweet. At times when fresh tomatoes are not abundant, tinned ones may be used instead. Other vegetables, whether mushrooms, aubergines, courgettes, sweet peppers, artichokes, peas, beans or olives, must be of good quality too.

To make a vegetable sauce, you nearly always start with a *soffritto*, that is, a mixture of chopped aromatic vegetables such as carrot, celery, onion or shallot, garlic and fresh herbs sautéed in olive oil, butter or other fat. It is useful to remember that if the recipe does not specify which type of fat to use, a vegetable oil is preferable, especially 'extra virgin' (the best quality) olive oil, or vegetable margarine made from groundnut (peanut), corn, coconut or palm oil.

All these elements are chosen, according to regional cooking traditions, because in combination they make a harmonious blend of tastes and colours.

There are also sauces where the predominant ingredients are herbs, such as basil (used in the delicious Genoese *pesto*), parsley, thyme, marjoram, rosemary, oregano and mint. Where a herb plays the leading role in a sauce it must, of course, be fresh; at other times it is possible to substitute dried herbs when just a little of their flavour is required. Among spices, spicy red chilli peppers are often used in vegetable sauces, either fresh, dried or powdered.

Vegetable sauces sometimes contain a little meat in the form of bacon or ham, for extra flavour, or fish, such as anchovies.

The recipes that follow will serve 6 as a first course or 4 as a main course.

Some ingredients for vegetable sauces, and commercial dried pasta (here, long and short fusilli)

Spaghetti with Rosemary

Time: 20 minutes
Ingredients
450 g (1 lb) spaghetti
6 to 7 tbsp olive oil
1 clove garlic, crushed
A sprig of freshly picked rosemary
1 300 g (10 oz) tin of peeled tomatoes
Salt

Heat the oil in a frying pan and add the garlic and rosemary. After a few minutes, add the tomatoes and simmer for a little longer.

Meanwhile, boil the spaghetti in a large saucepanful of salted water for about 10 minutes and drain when the pasta is *al dente*. Remove the garlic and rosemary from the sauce and pour the sauce over the spaghetti.

Hint: This dish does not require grated cheese and can be prepared in next to no time.

Spaghetti with Aubergine and Sweet Pepper Sauce

Time: 1½ hours
Ingredients
450 g (1 lb) spaghetti
500 g (1 lb 2 oz) ripe tomatoes
6 tbsp olive oil
1 onion, sliced
1 carrot, chopped
1 stick celery, chopped
1 tbsp chopped parsley
Salt and pepper
2 aubergines
2 sweet peppers
1 tbsp capers
60 g (2 oz) black olives, stoned and chopped
A bunch of fresh basil

Blanch the tomatoes in boiling water, peel them, remove the seeds and chop the flesh. Heat 2 tablespoons of oil in a pan over a gentle heat and sauté the onion for several minutes, stirring from time to time. Cover the pan when you are not stirring. Add the chopped carrot, celery and parsley. Stir in the tomatoes, salt and pepper and simmer for about 1 hour over a low heat.

Meanwhile, dice the aubergines and sweet peppers. Arrange the aubergines on a large dish and salt them; tilt the dish and leave for about 1 hour so that any bitter liquid drains away. Dry the aubergines with kitchen paper and fry them with the peppers in the remaining oil for about 10 minutes without adding any liquid.

Strain the tomato sauce and pour it back into its saucepan, adding the aubergines, peppers, capers and olives. Cover and simmer for another 20 minutes to blend all the flavours.

Boil the spaghetti in a large saucepanful of salted water, drain and pour the sauce over the pasta. Chop the basil and sprinkle it over just before serving.

Spaghetti with Aubergine and Sweet Pepper Sauce

Hint: Other vegetables in season, such as courgettes or green beans, may be added to the sauce.

Cold Summer Spaghetti

Time: 20 minutes
Ingredients
450 g (1 lb) very thin spaghetti
4 large ripe tomatoes, peeled,
  seeded and chopped
4 to 5 tbsp olive oil
2 tsp chopped fresh thyme or basil
Salt and pepper

Put the tomato pieces in a bowl and pour in a little oil, add the thyme (or basil), freshly ground pepper and salt.

Boil the spaghetti in salted water, drain when the pasta is *al dente,* rinse under cold water to cool and pour into a dish. Pour the remaining oil over and mix in the tomatoes.

Hint: You can improvise with this sauce and add other appetizing ingredients such as capers, slices of olive, slivers of sweet pepper, chunks of tuna fish, and so on.

Ceriole with Artichokes

Time: 45 minutes
Ingredients
450 g (1 lb) fresh ceriole (double
  pasta twists)
4 artichokes
1 small onion, chopped
1 stick celery, finely chopped
1 clove garlic, finely chopped
4 tbsp olive oil
A slice of lean bacon, about 1 cm
  ($\frac{1}{2}$ in) thick, diced
450 g (1 lb) ripe tomatoes, peeled,
  seeded and chopped
Salt and pepper
3 to 4 tbsp white wine
60 g (2 oz) smoked ham, chopped
1 bay leaf

Remove the artichokes' outer leaves and the bristles; wash and cut the artichokes into small pieces.

Sauté the chopped onion, celery and garlic in the oil, and as soon as the mixture begins to brown, add the bacon, the artichokes, the tomatoes, salt and pepper, and pour over the wine. As soon as the wine has evaporated, add the ham and the bay leaf and simmer for another 15 minutes.

Boil the ceriole in a large saucepanful of salted water, drain when the pasta is *al dente* and serve with the hot sauce, discarding the bay leaf first.

Hint: A 'Mediterranean' pasta dish which is rich and sustaining, serve it with a salad of raw vegetables with a dressing of olive oil, salt and pepper, and toasted wholewheat bread.

Ceriole with Artichokes

Maccheroni with Olives

Time: 30 minutes
Ingredients
450 g (1 lb) long smooth maccheroni
1 clove garlic
1 chilli pepper
4 to 5 tbsp olive oil
800 g (1¾ lb) tomatoes, peeled,
   seeded and chopped
Salt
100 g (3½ oz) black Gaeta olives
1 tbsp capers
1 tbsp chopped parsley

Crush the garlic and chilli pepper and sauté in the hot oil. Add the tomatoes together with salt; simmer for about 20 minutes. Remove the garlic and chilli. Remove the stones from the olives, chop the capers and add to the tomato sauce.

Break the maccheroni into lengths of about 7.5 cm (3 in) and boil in a large saucepanful of salted water. Drain when the pasta is *al dente* and serve with the sauce. Garnish with the chopped parsley and mix well.

Hint: The sauce can be made without the tomatoes; just use more oil.

Maccheroni Baked in Foil

Time: 30 minutes
Ingredients
450 g (1 lb) fluted maccheroni
450 g (1 lb) ripe tomatoes, peeled
   and seeded

200 g (7 oz) mozzarella cheese, diced
A bunch of fresh basil, chopped
30 g (1 oz) butter, cut into slivers
Salt and pepper

Cut the flesh of the tomatoes into strips and put in a bowl with the cubes of mozzarella, the basil, the butter and freshly ground pepper and mix well to make the sauce.

Boil the maccheroni in a large saucepanful of salted water and drain when the pasta is just *al dente* as it will continue cooking in the oven. Add the pasta to the sauce and mix carefully.

Preheat the oven to 180°C (350°F, mark 4). Lay two sheets of aluminium foil on the work surface and divide the pasta between the two sheets, placing it in the centre of each one. Fold up the sides to make a sealed packet and place on a baking tray. Bake in the oven for about 10 minutes. Transfer the foil parcels to a serving dish and unwrap the foil in front of everybody.

Hint: It is a good idea to adopt this method of cooking in aluminium foil because it requires little fat and allows the dish to retain its full flavour: during baking the aromas are sealed inside the foil envelope and absorbed by the pasta.

Maccheroni with Olives

Penne with Chilli

Time: 1 hour
Ingredients
450 g (1 lb) smooth penne
2 cloves garlic, crushed
5 to 6 tbsp olive oil
150 g (5 oz) button mushrooms,
    peeled and washed
Salt and pepper
A pinch of marjoram
3 tbsp dry white wine
600 g (1¼ lb) tomatoes, peeled,
    seeded and sliced
1 fresh red chilli pepper, sliced
60 g (2 oz) grated pecorino cheese

Sauté the garlic in half the hot oil and add the mushrooms, whole. Add salt and pepper and simmer for a few minutes. Sprinkle with marjoram and pour in the wine. When the wine has evaporated, add the tomatoes and simmer for about 30 minutes, stirring from time to time.

Boil the penne in a large saucepanful of salted water, drain when the pasta is *al dente* and transfer to a dish. Pour in more olive oil, add the tomato sauce, the sliced chilli pepper and the pecorino cheese. Mix well and serve at once.

Hint: If you don't like chilli pepper, substitute slices of fresh sweet red pepper.

Maccheroni with Mozzarella and Anchovies

Time: 1 hour
Ingredients
450 g (1 lb) very short fluted
    maccheroni
4 tbsp olive oil
1 clove garlic
1 400 g (14 oz) tin of peeled tomatoes
Salt and pepper
1 tsp sugar
60 g (2 oz) anchovy fillets, diced
200 g (7 oz) mozzarella cheese, diced

Heat 2 tablespoons of the oil in a saucepan, add the garlic and fry. Purée the tomatoes through a vegetable mill and add to the pan, together with salt, pepper and sugar. Cover, turn down the heat and simmer for about 45 minutes.

Boil the maccheroni in salted water and drain when the pasta is *al dente*. Pour into a dish and mix in the remaining oil at once, then stir in the anchovies and mozzarella. Pour the simmering sauce over the pasta and mix carefully.

Hint: Cut the mozzarella into very small pieces, or grate it coarsely, so that it melts as soon as it touches the hot pasta.

Maccheroni with Mozzarella and Anchovies

Rigatoni with Aromatic Herbs

Time: 1¼ hours
Ingredients
450 g (1 lb) rigatoni (large fluted
    dried pasta tubes)
450 g (1 lb) ripe tomatoes, peeled,
    seeded and chopped
A pinch of sugar
Salt and pepper
½ chilli pepper, chopped
6 tbsp olive oil
A small bunch of rocket lettuce
    (optional), chopped
A bunch of fresh parsley, chopped
A bunch of fresh basil, chopped
A small bunch of fresh sage,
    chopped
A sprig of fresh rosemary, chopped
1 tsp each marjoram, thyme and
    oregano
4 tbsp grated Parmesan cheese

Put the tomato pieces in a saucepan. Add the sugar, salt, pepper,
chilli pepper and 2 tablespoons of
the oil.

Simmer the sauce for about 1
hour over a low heat. Just before
removing the saucepan from the
heat, add all the herbs and lettuce
(if used) and stir.

Boil the rigatoni in a large
saucepanful of salted water, drain
when the pasta is *al dente* and
pour in the remaining olive oil.
Sprinkle with Parmesan and pour
half the sauce over the pasta. Mix
well, garnish with the rest of the
sauce and serve.

Hint: Always use fresh herbs
when they are in season; they are
much more aromatic. You can
substitute other herbs for the ones
in the recipe, depending on what
is available in the shops or in your
garden.

Cannolicchi with Ham and Tomato Sauce

Time: 30 minutes
Ingredients
450 g (1 lb) cannolicchi (small dried
    pasta tubes)
4 to 5 tbsp olive oil
1 small onion, finely chopped
1 tbsp each fresh parsley and basil
    chopped with 1 clove garlic
100 g (3½ oz) smoked ham, finely
    chopped
600 g (1¼ lb) fresh tomatoes, peeled,
    seeded and coarsely chopped
Salt and pepper
2 tbsp chopped basil

Heat the oil in a pan and sauté the
onion, parsley, basil and garlic.
After a minute or two add the
ham and sauté until it turns pale.
Add the tomatoes, salt and pepper and simmer for about 20
minutes.

Meanwhile, boil the cannolicchi in a large saucepanful of
salted water, drain when *al dente*
and serve with the boiling sauce.
Sprinkle with chopped basil.
Hint: To finish the dish, you can
add a handful of grated Parmesan.

Cannolicchi with Ham and Tomato Sauce

96

Trenette with Courgette Sauce

Time: 45 minutes
Ingredients
450 g (1 lb) trenette (thin noodles)
30 g (1 oz) butter
4 to 5 tbsp olive oil
1 small onion, finely chopped
1 stick celery, finely chopped
1 small carrot, finely chopped
800 g (1¾ lb) ripe tomatoes, peeled,
   seeded and chopped or 1 300 g
   (10 oz) tin of peeled tomatoes,
   chopped
Salt and pepper
1 egg
450 g (1 lb) courgettes, topped,
   tailed and washed, then sliced
2 to 3 tbsp flour
60 g (2 oz) grated Parmesan cheese

Heat the butter and 2 tablespoons of oil in a pan and sauté the onion, celery and carrot, then add the tomatoes, salt and pepper. Cover the pan and simmer for about 30 minutes, stirring often.

Break the egg into a bowl and beat it. Dip the courgette slices first in the egg and then in the flour and fry them in hot oil. Remove when they are golden brown and drain them on absorbent kitchen paper. Keep them hot.

Boil the trenette in a large saucepanful of salted water. Drain when the pasta is *al dente*, place in a dish and pour the hot sauce over. Cover with the courgettes and grated cheese. Mix and serve at once.

Hint: Cook this appetizing dish in the summer and when you can obtain new, sweet, tender courgettes.

Baked Pasta-Filled Tomatoes

Time: 1 hour 40 minutes
Ingredients
200 g (7 oz) short fluted maccheroni
8 large ripe tomatoes, preferably all
   the same size
Salt and pepper
150 g (5 oz) concentrated tomato
   purée
1 heaped tbsp basil chopped with
   1 clove garlic
4 to 5 tbsp olive oil

Slice the tops off the tomatoes horizontally and reserve them; remove and discard the seeds. Scoop out and reserve a little of the flesh, then turn the tomatoes upside-down on a plate to drain.

Boil the pasta in salted water and drain it when it is just *al dente*—remember, it will continue to cook in the oven.

Preheat the oven to 180°C (350°F, mark 4).

In a bowl, mix the reserved tomato flesh and about half the tomato purée with the chopped basil and garlic, salt and pepper and the boiled pasta. Mix carefully. Turn the tomatoes right

Baked Pasta-Filled Tomatoes

way up, sprinkle a little salt and olive oil over them and fill them with the pasta mixture. Do not fill them by more than two-thirds. Arrange them in an ovenproof dish and replace the tops on the tomatoes. Pour the rest of the tomato purée, diluted with a little water or, better still, stock, around the tomatoes.

Pour a little more oil over them and bake in the oven for about 40 minutes. Transfer the tomatoes to a heated plate and serve immediately or serve them straight from the ovenproof dish.

Hint: This is a new and interesting way of serving pasta. For the filling it is best to use types of small pasta which have a good 'resistance' to cooking (do not become over-cooked easily).

Ditaloni with Aubergines

Time: 1½ hours
Ingredients
450 g (1 lb) fluted ditaloni (large dried pasta tubes)
2 aubergines, washed and diced
Salt and pepper
4 tbsp olive oil
½ onion, sliced
½ tbsp chopped parsley
1 small carrot, chopped
1 stick celery, chopped
450 g (1 lb) ripe tomatoes, peeled, seeded and chopped or 1 300 g (10 oz) tin of peeled tomatoes, chopped
A bunch of fresh basil, chopped

Arrange the diced aubergine on a plate and add salt. Tilt the plate to allow the bitter juice to drain off and leave for 1 hour.

Meanwhile, prepare the sauce: heat 2 tablespoons of the oil in a pan and sauté the onion. Add the chopped parsley, carrot, celery, tomatoes, salt and pepper and stir well. Simmer for about 1 hour. You should obtain a thick sauce.

Dry the aubergine well (with kitchen paper) and fry in the remaining oil. Rub the tomato sauce through a nylon sieve and add the aubergine; simmer for another 15 minutes.

Meanwhile, boil the pasta in a large saucepan of salted water, drain when the pasta is *al dente* and serve with the sauce. Finish with the chopped basil.

Hint: Use either long, purple aubergines or the round variety, as long as they are firm and not too big.

Cold Ruote with Tomato Sauce

Time: 30 minutes
Ingredients
450 g (1 lb) ruote (dried pasta wheels)
300 g (10 oz) tomatoes, peeled and seeded
Salt and pepper
3 tbsp olive oil

1 tbsp parsley chopped with 1 clove garlic
1 tbsp chopped basil

Cut the flesh of the tomatoes into small pieces. Liquidize for a few seconds, or purée in a vegetable mill.

Boil the pasta in a large saucepanful of salted water, drain and cool under running cold water. Drain once more and pour into a deepish dish. Pour a little oil over the pasta at once. Add salt and pepper to the tomato sauce and pour it over the pasta, stirring well. Sprinkle over the parsley, garlic and basil, pepper and the remaining oil and serve cold.

Hint: Serve in summer when ripe, flavourful tomatoes are easy to obtain.

Ruote with Olives and Capers

Time: 40 minutes
Ingredients
450 g (1 lb) ruote (dried pasta wheels)
1 sweet green pepper
1 small onion, chopped
75 g (2½ oz) smoked bacon, diced
2 tbsp olive oil
450 g (1 lb) ripe tomatoes, peeled, seeded and chopped
60 g (2 oz) each green and black olives, stoned and sliced
A pinch of oregano
1 tbsp capers
Salt and pepper

Hold the sweet pepper on the end of a fork over the gas flame to blister the skin. Rub with a cloth to remove the skin. Then, cut the pepper open, remove the seeds and cut the flesh into strips.

Sauté the onion and bacon in a little hot oil; when the bacon begins to brown, add the strips of pepper and let them soften. Then add the tomatoes, the olives, the oregano, the capers and a little salt and pepper. Simmer the sauce for about 20 minutes or until it thickens.

Boil the ruote in a large saucepanful of salted water, drain when the pasta is *al dente* and serve with the hot sauce.

Hint: Do not add cheese to this dish. This sauce goes equally well with other types of short pasta, such as fusilli and conchiglie.

Tagliatelle with Cheesy Onion Sauce

Time: 45 minutes
Ingredients
450 g (1 lb) fresh or dried tagliatelle
90 g (3 oz) butter
450 g (1 lb) onions, sliced
10 g (⅓ oz) flour
100 g (3½ oz) grated Gruyère cheese
½ litre (18 fl oz) milk
Salt

Heat 60 g (2 oz) of the butter in a pan. Add the onions, cover and cook over a low heat for about 20

minutes. The onion should cook, but not brown. Stir frequently. Mix in the flour and cook for a few more minutes.

Stir in the grated Gruyère, mix well and dilute by pouring in the milk a little at a time. Bring to the boil, add salt and simmer, stirring constantly, for about 10 minutes.

Boil the tagliatelle in a large saucepanful of boiling water, drain when the pasta is *al dente* and pour into a preheated dish containing the remaining butter, cut in pieces. Mix carefully, cover with the onion sauce and serve at once.

Hint: If they have a very strong flavour, the onions can be blanched in boiling salted water for a few minutes after slicing.

Tagliatelle with Tomato and Herb Sauce

Time: 1 hour
Ingredients
450 g (1 lb) fresh or dried tagliatelle
800 g (1¾ lb) very ripe tomatoes, peeled and seeded
Salt
A pinch of thyme
2 bay leaves
A pinch of sugar
4 tbsp olive oil

Crush the tomatoes and put them in a saucepan. Add a few pinches of salt, the thyme, bay leaves and sugar and simmer until the sauce has reduced and thickened. Then, rub it through a nylon sieve and remove the bay leaves. Mix in 2 tablespoons of olive oil when the cooking is over.

Boil the tagliatelle in a large saucepanful of salted water, drain when the pasta is *al dente* and pour into a dish. Pour the remaining olive oil over the tagliatelle followed by the tomato sauce.

Hint: This delicate pasta dish is particularly suitable for those with sensitive stomachs as the sauce is simple and made without a *soffritto* (base of sautéed onion, celery and carrot).

Green Tagliatelle with Mushrooms and Peas

Time: 1 hour 40 minutes
Ingredients
450 g (1 lb) fresh or dried green tagliatelle
3 tbsp olive oil
30 g (1 oz) butter
½ small onion, finely chopped
100 g (3½ oz) smoked ham or bacon, ½ fat and ½ lean, finely chopped
150 g (5 oz) button mushrooms, peeled, washed and sliced
Salt and pepper
500 g (1 lb 2 oz) fresh tomatoes, peeled and put through a vegetable mill
150 g (5 oz) fresh shelled or frozen peas
60 g (2 oz) grated Parmesan cheese

Tomato and Herb Sauce

Heat the olive oil and a knob of butter in a pan and sauté the onion and ham. Add the mushrooms, salt and pepper and, after 5 minutes, the tomatoes. Simmer over a low heat, stirring frequently.

Boil the peas separately in a little water or, better still, stock, and add them 10 minutes before removing the pan from the cooker.

Boil the tagliatelle in salted water, drain when the pasta is *al dente* and pour it into a soup tureen that has been warmed by having boiling water poured into it, and then dried. Pour the mushroom and pea sauce over the tagliatelle and stir in the remaining butter and the cheese. **Hint:** Use fresh peas when in season; they are sweeter and more delicate in flavour.

Fazzoletti with Basil Cream Sauce

Time: 25 minutes
Ingredients
450 g (1 lb) fazzoletti (small squares of fresh egg pasta) or packet lasagne
A large bunch of fresh basil
1 or 2 cloves garlic
200 ml (7 fl oz) single cream
60 g (2 oz) grated Parmesan cheese
Salt and white pepper
30 g (1 oz) butter

Wash and dry the basil leaves, and liquidize with the garlic and a few tablespoons of cream; this should give you a soft, smooth cream. Make a similar paste with the cheese and a few more tablespoons of cream by liquidizing them together for a few seconds.

Boil the fazzoletti in a large saucepanful of salted water. Meanwhile, heat the butter with the remaining cream and add the liquidized cheese mixture. Drain the pasta when it is *al dente,* pour it into a dish and pour over the cheese sauce and finally, the basil mixture. Mix carefully and serve. **Hint:** Make lots of basil cream and serve some of it separately in a sauceboat. It is good with gnocchi as well.

Home-Made Lasagne with Basil Sauce

Time: $1\frac{1}{4}$ hours
Ingredients
For the pasta:
400 g (14 oz) strong flour
4 eggs
Salt
For the sauce:
5 bunches of fresh basil or about 200 g (7 oz)
2 cloves garlic
1 tbsp pine nuts
A pinch of marjoram
60 g (2 oz) grated Parmesan cheese
Salt
60 ml (2 fl oz) olive oil

Prepare the egg pasta as described on page 21. Roll out the dough very thinly and, using a pastry wheel, cut out rounds which are slightly smaller in diameter than the dish in which you intend to serve the pasta. Arrange the rounds of pasta on the floured pastry board.

Wash the basil leaves, drain, dry and chop them together with the garlic and the pine nuts. Put the mixture in a bowl and add the marjoram, cheese, and a pinch of salt then slowly pour in the oil. Mix again.

Boil the rounds of pasta, one at a time, for a few minutes, in salted water. Drain and dry them with a tea-towel and arrange them in a preheated serving dish, alternating each layer with a layer of basil sauce.

Hint: To save time, make the basil sauce in a liquidizer and add 2 or 3 extra tablespoons of oil.

Tagliatelle with Onion Sauce

Time: 1¼ hours
Ingredients
450 g (1 lb) fresh or dried tagliatelle
450 g (1 lb) onions
Salt
60 g (2 oz) butter
10 g (⅓ oz) flour
100 g (3½ oz) grated Gruyère cheese
450 ml (¾ pint) milk

Peel and slice the onions and parboil them in salted water for a few minutes. Drain well and place in a frying pan with butter. Cover and cook over a gentle heat for about 30 minutes, stirring often. Mix in the flour and continue cooking for a few minutes. Add the Gruyère. Bring the milk to the boil and add to the sauce, a little at a time. Add salt and cover again. Simmer over a low heat for another 10 minutes.

Boil the tagliatelle in a large saucepanful of salted water and drain when the pasta is *al dente*. Pour into a serving dish and cover with the onion sauce.

Hint: If you like you can place the sauce-topped pasta, in an ovenproof dish, in a hot oven for 20 minutes to brown the surface lightly.

Tagliatelle Soufflé

Time: 1 hour
Ingredients
300 g (10 oz) fresh or dried tagliatelle
Salt and pepper
1.5 litres (1¾ pints) milk
60 g (2 oz) butter
2 eggs

Boil the tagliatelle in the lightly salted milk.

Meanwhile, beat the butter with a spoon until it is creamy

and add the egg yolks one at a time, a pinch of pepper and about 125 ml (4 fl oz) of the boiling milk.

Preheat the oven to 180°C (350°F, mark 4).

Drain the tagliatelle when the pasta is *al dente* (you can reserve the remaining milk for use in a soup or sauce) and pour the pasta into the dish containing the beaten eggs. Beat the egg whites until stiff and fold them into the other ingredients. Butter an oven-proof dish and pour in the tagliatelle mixture. Bake until the surface begins to brown—about 30-40 minutes. Remove from the oven, leave for a few minutes and serve.

Hint: To test whether the soufflé is cooked all the way through, plunge a toothpick or knife blade into the centre; the filling should be set and not still liquid.

Baked Maccheroni

Time: 45 minutes
Ingredients
450 g (1 lb) short fluted maccheroni
300 g (10 oz) mushrooms
1 clove garlic
2 tbsp olive oil
175 ml (6 fl oz) home-made tomato
   sauce
Salt and pepper
60 g (2 oz) butter
60 g (2 oz) grated Parmesan cheese
100 g (3½ oz) fontina cheese, diced

100 g (3½ oz) lean ham, diced
2 eggs, beaten

Wipe the mushrooms and slice them thinly. Brown the whole clove of garlic in the oil and add the mushrooms. Sauté them and then add the tomato sauce; simmer until the mushrooms are cooked.

Meanwhile, boil the maccheroni in a large saucepanful of salted water. Drain when the pasta is *al dente*, reserving a little of the cooking liquid.

Preheat the oven to 180°C (350°F, mark 4).

Put 40 g (1½ oz) of the butter in small knobs in the bottom of an ovenproof dish with the Parmesan and fontina cheeses and the ham. Mix well, add the maccheroni and a little of the water they were cooked in. Pour in the beaten eggs, add pepper and mix again. Sprinkle with knobs of the remaining butter. Bake in the oven for 15-20 minutes.

Remove the garlic clove from the mushroom and tomato sauce. Serve the sauce with the baked pasta.

Hint: This dish contains eggs, cheese and ham, making it a substantial meal. A salad of raw vegetables is recommended to complete the menu.

Baked Maccheroni

106

Home-Made Cappieddi with Mushroom Sauce

Time: 1¼ hours
Ingredients
For the pasta:
400 g (14 oz) strong flour
4 eggs
A pinch of salt
For the sauce:
4 tbsp olive oil
1 medium-sized onion, finely sliced
60 g (2 oz) smoked ham, diced
1 clove garlic
300 g (10 oz) fresh mushrooms
400 g (14 oz) fresh or tinned peeled
   tomatoes
A bunch of fresh basil
A bunch of fresh parsley
Salt and pepper
60 g (2 oz) grated Parmesan cheese

Mix the flour, eggs and salt to a dough as described on page 21. Roll out the dough in a thin sheet and, using a serrated pastry wheel or a knife, cut out little squares. Fold them in half, diagonally, making each one look like a little hat. Lay them out on the pastry board to dry, keeping them well apart.

Heat the oil in a pan and soften the onion, ham and whole clove of garlic. Wipe the mushrooms with a damp cloth, cut off the base of the stalks, slice them and add to the pan; simmer for a few minutes. Then add the tomatoes. Tie the bunches of basil and parsley together with kitchen string before putting them into the pan with the other ingredients. Add salt and freshly ground pepper. Simmer for 35-40 minutes.

Boil the pasta in a large saucepanful of salted water, drain when it is *al dente,* transfer to a serving dish and pour the sauce over it. Remove the herbs and the garlic before serving the dish with the cheese.

Hint: To save time, use commercial dried farfalle (butterflies) instead of home-made cappieddi.

Malloreddus with Tomato Sauce

Time: 1 hour
Ingredients
450 g (1 lb) fresh or dried
   malloreddus (see page 48)
60 g (2 oz) bacon, chopped
1 small onion, sliced
4 tbsp olive oil
1 clove garlic, crushed
A few basil leaves
800 g (1¾ lb) fresh tomatoes, peeled,
   seeded and chopped
½ beef stock cube or ¼ tsp beef
   extract
Salt and pepper
75 g (2½ oz) grated pecorino cheese

Soften the bacon and onion in the hot oil. Add the garlic, basil and, after a few minutes, the tomatoes. Dissolve the stock cube in a little hot water and add to the pan with

Malloreddus with Tomato Sauce

the salt and pepper; simmer for about 45 minutes or until a thick sauce is obtained.

Boil the malloreddus in a large saucepanful of salted water, drain when *al dente* and serve with the hot sauce and the cheese.

Hint: If you are using dried pasta, add a tiny pinch of saffron to the water to brighten the colour.

Trofie with Basil Sauce

Time: $1\frac{3}{4}$ hours
Ingredients
450 g (1 lb) fresh trofie (see page 50)
2 bunches of fresh basil
1 clove garlic
1 tbsp pine nuts
Salt
125 ml (4 fl oz) olive oil
1 tbsp grated pecorino cheese
1 tbsp grated Parmesan cheese

Wash the basil leaves and lay them on a tea-towel to dry. Then put them in a mortar with the garlic, pine nuts and a pinch of salt. Crush against the bottom and sides of the mortar with the pestle until you obtain a paste. Add the oil, a little at a time, and finally, combine the pecorino and the Parmesan cheeses and add them to the mixture.

Boil the trofie in a large saucepanful of salted water, drain when *al dente* and serve at once with a generous amount of sauce.

Hint: You can vary the basil sauce by adding crushed walnuts or, if you want a spicy hot flavour, a pinch of chilli powder.

Wholewheat Spaghetti with Vegetable Sauce

Time: 30 minutes
Ingredients
450 g (1 lb) wholewheat spaghetti
1 small onion, finely chopped
1 clove garlic, finely chopped
4 to 5 tbsp olive oil
$\frac{1}{2}$ sweet red or yellow pepper
350 g (12 oz) fresh or tinned peeled tomatoes, rubbed through a sieve
Salt and pepper
100 g ($3\frac{1}{2}$ oz) stuffed olives, sliced into rounds
1 tbsp chopped parsley

Sauté the onion and garlic in the hot oil. Scorch the sweet pepper over a flame and peel off the skin. Slice the flesh and sauté with the onion for a few minutes. Then add the tomatoes, salt, pepper and the sliced olives (reserving a few for garnish). Continue simmering, stirring from time to time. Before removing the sauce from the cooker, add the parsley.

Boil the spaghetti, drain when the pasta is *al dente* and serve with the sauce. Garnish with the remaining olives and serve at once.

Trofie with Basil Sauce

Hint: This type of sauce doesn't usually require the addition of cheese.

Wholewheat Spaghetti with Anchovy and Capers

Time: 30 minutes
Ingredients
450 g (1 lb) wholewheat spaghetti
5 to 6 tbsp olive oil
1 tbsp chopped parsley
1 clove garlic, chopped
A few anchovy fillets in oil, drained and cut into strips
300 g (10 oz) ripe tomatoes, chopped
1 tbsp concentrated tomato purée
Salt and pepper
1 tbsp capers, rinsed and sliced

Heat the oil in a saucepan. Add the chopped parsley, garlic and anchovy and sauté over a low heat. Add the tomato pieces to the pan, dilute the tomato purée with a little water and pour in, and season with salt and pepper. When the sauce thickens, add the capers and leave to simmer for a few minutes more.

Boil the pasta in a large saucepanful of salted water, drain when it is *al dente* and serve with the sauce.

Hint: You can garnish the dish with additional anchovy fillets.

Spaghetti with Marrow Flowers and Basil

Time: 40 minutes
Ingredients
450 g (1 lb) thin spaghetti
400 g (14 oz) ripe tomatoes
1 small white onion, sliced
1 clove garlic
3 to 4 tbsp olive oil
About 10 very fresh marrow flowers, pistils removed, washed and coarsely sliced
A few basil leaves
Salt and pepper

Blanch the tomatoes in boiling water, peel and put them through a vegetable mill.

Soften the onion and the whole clove of garlic in the hot oil and add the marrow flowers. Fry until they wilt and then add the tomatoes and whole basil leaves and continue cooking until the sauce has thickened. At the end, discard the garlic and basil leaves.

Boil the spaghetti in a large saucepanful of salted water, drain when the pasta is *al dente,* pour into a dish and add the sauce. Mix with care, add a little more freshly ground pepper and garnish with a few basil leaves.

Hint: Do not add cheese as this would smother the delicate flavour of the fresh flowers.

Spaghetti with Marrow Flowers and Basil

Maccheroni with Garlic, Oil and Parsley

Time: 20 minutes
Ingredients
450 g (1 lb) long smooth maccheroni
Salt
100 ml (3 fl oz) olive oil
3 cloves garlic, crushed
1 fresh chilli pepper, chopped
A small bunch of fresh parsley

Divide the maccheroni into pieces about 10 cm (4 in) long, boil in salted water and drain when the pasta is *al dente*.

Heat the oil and sauté the garlic. Stir in the chilli pepper and cook briefly so the oil absorbs the flavours. Toss the sauce over the maccheroni, sprinkle with the parsley, mix and serve.

Hint: This very quick dish is also good cold.

Maccheroni with Garlic, Oil and Parsley

PASTA WITH FISH SAUCES

Fresh fish, crustaceans, shellfish, good-quality olive oil, white and black pepper and many different herbs are the basic ingredients for fish sauces.

It is essential to start with a *soffritto* (sautéed mixture) of garlic or onion in oil, and to add natural aromatic herbs and spices. The most commonly used are parsley, basil, oregano, mint and wild thyme.

There are many different fish sauces—cooked or uncooked, with or without tomatoes—all equally appetizing and quick. All that is required is a balanced choice of ingredients. The secrets for an excellent sauce are few but essential: very fresh fish, preferably straight from the water, fresh herbs and the appropriate pasta should be used. No part of the fish should be wasted; the water inside shellfish as well as the *fumet* (the liquid obtained by poaching fish scraps or shells in water and wine) can be added to the sauce (after boiling to reduce it and straining) to enhance the flavour.

Long dried pasta shapes are recommended with fish sauces; for example, bucatini, spaghetti, zite, maccheroni and fusilli.

The recipes that follow will serve 6 as a first course or 4 as a main course.

Some ingredients for fish sauces, and commercial dried pasta (here, long fusilli and long maccheroni or zite)

117

Fusilli with Eels

Time: 1 hour
Ingredients
300 g (10 oz) fusilli
300 g (10 oz) tiny eels
4 tbsp flour
4 tbsp olive oil
1 small onion, chopped
1 clove garlic (optional)
800 g (1¾ lb) fresh young peas
Salt and pepper
3 to 4 tbsp dry white wine
500 g (1 lb 2 oz) ripe tomatoes,
    peeled, seeded and chopped
1 tbsp chopped parsley

Gut the eels and cut into pieces without removing the skin. Wash, dry and flour the pieces.

Heat the olive oil and sauté the onion. Add a whole clove of garlic if you wish. Add the peas and simmer for about 10 minutes, adding a little water. Put in the eel pieces, salt and pepper, and brown them. After a few minutes, pour in the white wine and simmer until it has almost all evaporated. At this point add the tomatoes and a little water.

Simmer, stirring from time to time, until both the peas and the fish are tender and cooked through.

Ten minutes before removing the eels from the heat, boil the fusilli in a large saucepanful of salted water, drain when the pasta is *al dente* and pour a little of the sauce over. Pour the pasta into the middle of a deep serving or earthenware dish, arrange the eels around the edge, pour the rest of the sauce over and garnish with parsley.

Hint: Serve as a main course followed simply by a selection of cheeses.

Bucatini with Hake

Time: 45 minutes
Ingredients
450 g (1 lb) bucatini
1 hake weighing about 400 g (14 oz)
4 tbsp olive oil
1 small onion, chopped
Salt and pepper
3 to 4 tbsp dry white wine
300 g (10 oz) peeled tomatoes,
    rubbed through a sieve
1 tbsp parsley chopped with 1 clove
    garlic

Gut the hake, make a lengthways cut and, using a sharp pointed knife, fillet the fish. Wash and dry thoroughly with kitchen paper.

Heat the oil in a frying pan and sauté the onion. Cut the hake fillets into pieces before adding them to the pan. Add salt and pepper and brown the fish. Pour a few tablespoons of white wine over and allow it to evaporate. Then add the tomatoes and simmer gently, until the sauce thickens.

Meanwhile, boil the bucatini in a large saucepanful of salted

Fusilli with Eels

118

water and drain when the pasta is *al dente*. Pour into a deep dish. Add the chopped parsley to the sauce at the last moment and pour over the bucatini.

Hint: Do not serve any kind of cheese with this dish, not even pungent varieties.

Bucatini alla Marinara

Time: $1\frac{1}{4}$ hours
Ingredients
450 g (1 lb) bucatini
30 g (1 oz) dried mushrooms
1 clove garlic
A few sage leaves
100 ml (3 fl oz) olive oil
1 onion, chopped
1 carrot, chopped
1 stick celery, chopped
125 ml (4 fl oz) dry white wine
100 g ($3\frac{1}{2}$ oz) squid, cut into small
    pieces
100 g ($3\frac{1}{2}$ oz) shrimps
60 ml (2 fl oz) brandy
A tiny pinch of saffron
$\frac{1}{2}$ tsp curry powder
1 400 g (14 oz) tin of peeled tomatoes
100 g ($3\frac{1}{2}$ oz) shelled mussels
100 g ($3\frac{1}{2}$ oz) shelled clams
Salt and pepper
1 tbsp chopped parsley

Soak the mushrooms in warm water.

Sauté the garlic and sage leaves in the hot oil; remove them and put in the onion, carrot and celery and soften for a couple of minutes. Add the white wine and allow it to evaporate. Drain the mushrooms and add them, together with the squid pieces. Simmer over a low heat for about 10 minutes, then add the shrimps and the brandy. Dissolve the saffron and curry powder in a little of the sauce and add them to the other ingredients together with the tomatoes. Cover the pan and simmer until the sauce thickens.

About 10 minutes before removing the pan from the heat, add the mussels and clams. Season the sauce to taste and, finally, sprinkle with chopped parsley.

Boil the bucatini in a large saucepanful of salted water, drain when the pasta is *al dente* and pour over half the sauce. Arrange on a serving dish and pour over the rest of the sauce.

Hint: Add the shellfish at the last minute and avoid overcooking them otherwise they will become rubbery. Keep some of the water from the mussels and clams and add it to the sauce to enhance the flavour.

Maritime Spaghetti

Time: $1\frac{1}{2}$ hours
Ingredients
450 g (1 lb) spaghetti
500 g (1 lb 2 oz) fresh clams
5 tbsp olive oil
2 cloves garlic, finely chopped

500 g (1 lb 2 oz) ripe tomatoes or
  1 250 g (9 oz) tin of tomatoes,
  peeled and rubbed through a
  nylon sieve
Salt and pepper
200 g (7 oz) octopus, cleaned and
  thinly sliced
200 g (7 oz) shrimps, peeled
1 heaped tbsp chopped parsley

Scrub the clams and heat them in a small frying pan over a moderate heat to open the shells. Remove the clams from the shells as they open and reserve the liquid that collects in the pan.

Heat 2 tablespoons of the oil and sauté the garlic. Add the tomatoes, salt and freshly ground pepper and let the sauce simmer until it thickens.

In a separate saucepan, heat the rest of the oil, put in the octopus slices, salt and pepper, and cook for about 15 minutes. Then add the shrimps to the octopus. Strain the liquid from the clams and add to the octopus and shrimps. Continue simmering. Just before removing the sauce from the heat, add the clams to the pan.

Boil the spaghetti in a large saucepanful of salted water and drain when the pasta is *al dente*. Place in a preheated serving dish and pour the tomato sauce over the pasta. Then pour on the fish with their sauce. Sprinkle generously with chopped parsley.

Hint: Do not serve cheese with this dish. If necessary, add a little dry white wine or stock to the octopus during cooking.

Spaghetti with Cuttlefish

Time: $1\frac{1}{4}$ hours
Ingredients
450 g (1 lb) spaghetti
4 cuttlefish
5 to 6 tbsp olive oil
1 small onion, finely chopped
1 carrot, finely chopped
1 stick celery, finely chopped
1 clove garlic, finely chopped
A bunch of fresh parsley, chopped
Salt
Chilli powder
500 g (1 lb 2 oz) ripe tomatoes or
  1 250 g (9 oz) tin of peeled
  tomatoes, rubbed through a
  nylon sieve

Remove the hard beak-like part of the cuttlefish, the eyes and the ink sacs. Dip the cuttlefish in boiling water for a second and drain. Peel off the outer skin and cut the flesh into thin slices.

Heat the oil and add the chopped onion, carrot, celery, garlic and half the parsley. Sauté, then add the cuttlefish slices, salt, a generous pinch of chilli powder and the tomatoes. Cover and simmer until the cuttlefish is tender.

Boil the spaghetti in a large saucepanful of salted water, drain when the pasta is *al dente,* serve with the sauce and sprinkle the remaining parsley on top.

Hint: If the sauce thickens too much before the cuttlefish are cooked, add a little water or dry white wine.

Spaghetti with Tiny Mussels

Time: 1 hour
Ingredients
450 g (1 lb) spaghetti
1 kg (2¼ lb) fresh tiny mussels or 200 g (7 oz) tinned or frozen mussels
2 cloves garlic, crushed
4 tbsp olive oil
350 g (12 oz) peeled tomatoes, chopped
Salt and pepper
A large bunch of fresh parsley, chopped

Scrub the mussels thoroughly under running water, drain well and place in a large frying pan over a moderate heat. Leave until they open, stirring occasionally with a wooden spoon. Put a few mussels to one side and remove the others from their shells. Strain the liquid which has collected in the pan (it will have a 'sea' flavour) through a sieve lined with a piece of muslin, and reserve the liquid.

Boil the spaghetti in a large saucepanful of salted water. Meanwhile, sauté the garlic in the oil. When it begins to brown, add the liquid from the mussels, the tomatoes, salt and pepper. Simmer over a high heat until the sauce thickens. Then add the mussels, stir, and remove from the heat.

Drain the spaghetti when it is *al dente,* pour into a preheated serving dish and serve with the mussel sauce. Sprinkle the chopped parsley on top and garnish with the mussels in their shells set aside earlier.

Hint: If you use tinned mussels (but not mussels in vinegar), add the liquid they come in to the sauce, even though the flavour will not be so strong. You can also make the mussel sauce without tomatoes, using more oil.

Linguine with Mussel Sauce

Time: 1¼ hours
Ingredients
450 g (1 lb) linguine
1 kg (2¼ lb) mussels
125 ml (4 fl oz) dry white wine
3 tbsp olive oil
1 shallot or small onion, chopped
1 clove garlic, chopped
1 piece of fresh chilli pepper, sliced
500 g (1 lb 2 oz) ripe tomatoes, peeled and put through a vegetable mill
1 tbsp capers
Salt and pepper
A bunch of fresh parsley, chopped

Spaghetti with Tiny Mussels

122

Scrub the mussels and wash them thoroughly under running water. Put them in a large frying pan, pour over the wine and heat until the shells open. Remove the mussels from their shells and set them aside together with the liquid which collected in the bottom of the pan. Reduce and strain this liquid.

Heat the oil and soften the shallot, garlic and chilli pepper. After a few minutes, add the tomatoes, capers, salt and pepper and continue to simmer over a high heat. Five minutes before the sauce is reduced enough to be removed from the heat, add the liquid from the mussels and then the mussels. Simmer for 2 minutes, remove from the heat and add the chopped parsley.

Boil the linguine in a large saucepanful of salted water, drain when the pasta is *al dente* and serve with the sauce.

Hint: Do not serve cheese with this dish. To ensure that the mussels are fresh and alive to begin with, check that the shells are either firmly closed or only slightly open. If one is slightly open, it should snap shut when touched. Discard any mussels that do not close. Conversely, after heating the mussels in the frying pan, discard any that have not opened.

Bucatini with Prawns and Clams

Time: $1\frac{1}{4}$ hours
Ingredients
450 g (1 lb) spaghetti
200 g (7 oz) large raw prawns or cooked prawns
200 g (7 oz) raw shrimps or cooked shrimps
1 bay leaf
800 g ($1\frac{3}{4}$ lb) clams
3 tbsp brandy
1 small onion, chopped
1 clove garlic, chopped
4 tbsp olive oil
400 g (14 oz) tomatoes, peeled and chopped
Salt and pepper

If the prawns and shrimps are raw, boil them in a little water with the bay leaf. Heat the clams in a frying pan to open the shells and, as they open, remove the clams from the shells and reserve the liquid that has collected in the bottom of the frying pan.

Peel the shrimps and prawns and keep both their cooking water and their shells. Mix the strained cooking liquid from the clams with that from the shrimps and prawns. Crush the shrimp and prawn shells and add them, together with the brandy. Reduce the fish stock over a high heat for about 15 minutes and strain through a sieve lined with muslin.

Fry the onion and garlic in 2 tablespoons of the oil and add the

Bucatini with Prawns and Clams

124

tomatoes. Pour in the strained fish stock, add salt and pepper and simmer over a moderate heat until the sauce thickens.

Meanwhile, boil the spaghetti in a large saucepanful of salted water. Add the clams, shrimps and prawns to the sauce and allow the flavours to blend for a few minutes. Drain the pasta when it is *al dente* and serve with the remaining oil and the piping hot sauce.

Hint: Shellfish are generally added to the sauce at the last minute, otherwise, if they are overcooked, they become hard and rubbery.

Maccheroni with Prawns

Time: $1\frac{1}{4}$ hours
Ingredients
450 g (1 lb) long smooth maccheroni
A sprig of fresh parsley
1 bay leaf
1 stick celery
A few peppercorns
Salt
800 g ($1\frac{3}{4}$ lb) large raw prawns
100 ml (3 fl oz) olive oil
1 or 2 cloves garlic
A small piece of fresh chilli pepper, shredded
600 g ($1\frac{1}{4}$ lb) ripe tomatoes, peeled, seeded and chopped
1 tbsp chopped parsley

Fill a large saucepan with water and add the sprig of parsley, the bay leaf, celery, peppercorns and salt and bring to the boil. Wash the prawns and immerse them in the boiling water for 3 to 4 minutes. Drain, remove the transparent shells along the backs, the heads and tips of the tails. Reserve a few unpeeled prawns for garnish, and cut the rest into pieces.

Break the maccheroni into 10 cm (4 in) lengths (or longer if you prefer) and boil in a large saucepanful of salted water.

Heat the oil and brown the whole cloves of garlic. Add the chilli, tomatoes and salt; simmer for 10 to 15 minutes until the sauce has thickened. Add the prawns and continue simmering for a very short time.

Drain the maccheroni when the pasta is *al dente,* pour the sauce over the maccheroni and transfer to a serving dish. Sprinkle with the chopped parsley. Garnish with the whole prawns.

Hint: To enhance the flavour of the sauce, press the prawn shells in a sieve and add the result, even though there may not be much, to the sauce.

Torciglioni with Tuna

Time: 30 minutes
Ingredients
450 g (1 lb) torciglioni (dried pasta twists)
1 clove garlic, crushed
5 to 6 tbsp olive oil

100 g (3½ oz) tinned tuna in oil,
   crushed with a fork
300 g (10 oz) fresh tomatoes, peeled
   and rubbed through a sieve
Salt and pepper
A pinch of oregano

Sauté the garlic in the oil over a moderate heat. Remove the garlic and put in the tuna and, after a few minutes, the tomatoes. Add salt and oregano and continue simmering until the sauce thickens.

Meanwhile, boil the torciglioni in a large saucepanful of salted water, drain when *al dente* and serve with the tuna sauce, seasoned with plenty of freshly ground pepper.

Hint: To make a lighter dish, use less oil and drain the oil from the tinned tuna.

Penne with Smoked Salmon

Time: 45 minutes
Ingredients
450 g (1 lb) penne
15 g (½ oz) butter
15 g (½ oz) flour
200 ml (7 fl oz) milk, heated
100 g (3½ oz) grated Parmesan
   cheese
150 ml (5 fl oz) single cream
150 g (5 oz) smoked salmon, thinly
   sliced
Salt

Melt the butter in a saucepan and add the flour, stirring well. Add the hot milk, little by little, to obtain a smooth béchamel sauce. Remove from the heat and stir in the Parmesan cheese and the cream. Leave to cool. Rub half the salmon through a sieve and stir it into the sauce.

Boil the penne in salted water and drain when the pasta is *al dente*. Meanwhile, preheat the oven to 200°C (400°F, mark 6). Pour the penne into an ovenproof dish and cover with the salmon sauce. Top with the remaining salmon slices and put in the oven for about 10 minutes.

Hint: Fish does not always go well with cheese. In this case, however, you can combine them as the delicate flavour of the sophisticated sauce will not be spoiled.

Tagliolini with Caviare

Time: 25 minutes
Ingredients
450 g (1 lb) fresh or dried tagliolini
Salt
2 small tins of Russian caviare
A little lemon juice
60 g (2 oz) butter

Boil the tagliolini in a large saucepanful of salted water. Meanwhile, sprinkle the caviare with lemon juice and cut the butter into small pieces.

Drain the pasta when it is *al dente* and keep back 2 tablespoons of the water it was cooked in. Pour the tagliolini into a preheated serving dish, pour over the cooking water and add the butter and caviare. Stir carefully and serve.

Hint: It is advisable to use best-quality caviare if you really wish to savour this delicate and unusual pasta dish. German caviare is also recommended.

Maccheroni with Sardines

Time: 1 hour
Ingredients
450 g (1 lb) maccheroni
30 g (1 oz) sultanas
500 g (1 lb 2 oz) fresh sardines
1 onion, chopped
100 ml (3 fl oz) olive oil
4 anchovy fillets, crushed to a paste
A pinch of fennel seeds
A pinch of saffron
30 g (1 oz) pine nuts
30 g (1 oz) butter

Soak the sultanas in warm water. Rinse, cut open and remove the bones from the sardines.

Sauté the onion in half the oil and add half the sardines and the anchovy paste. Stir, and add the fennel seeds and saffron. Drain the sultanas and add to the other ingredients together with the pine nuts and a little water to make a sauce which is not too thick. Stir

the sauce to blend the ingredients.

Fry the remaining sardines in the rest of the oil until they are golden brown. Preheat the oven to 180°C (350°F, mark 4).

Boil the maccheroni in a large saucepanful of salted water, drain when the pasta is *al dente* and pour over half the sauce. Butter an ovenproof dish and pour in the maccheroni. Top with the fried sardines and pour over the rest of the sauce. Place in the oven for about 10 minutes.

Hint: The sultanas make this a rather unusual recipe; if they do not appeal to your taste you can omit them and use more anchovies.

Some ingredients for Maccheroni with Sardines

128

PASTA WITH WHITE SAUCES

White sauces for pasta are made with a few rich ingredients: butter, milk, cream and cheese with the occasional addition of egg yolks. Their hallmark is delicacy of flavour.

Tomatoes and herbs, with few exceptions, disappear to make way for fresh cheeses like mozzarella, ricotta and mascherpone, matured cheeses like Parmesan and other hard or semi-hard cheeses such as fontina, Gruyère and Emmenthal. They are always added (the soft and semi-hard cheeses, that is) cut into tiny slivers or coarsely grated so that they will melt easily in a *bain-marie* over a low heat.

Olive oil plays a lesser role too and is replaced by top-quality fresh butter and cream. The cream most recommended for these sauces is single cream. It should be added at the last minute so that it will blend perfectly with the other ingredients.

Other special ingredients include nuts, delicate meats and shellfish, spices and, for the ultimate in luxury, the rare fragrance of truffles. Not all the sauces in the section are necessarily 'white' in colour, nor is the term 'white' sauce synonymous with 'light' in texture. Classic 'white sauces' of milk and cream added to a roux base of butter and flour are described as béchamel sauces throughout this book.

The recipes that follow will serve 6 as a first course or 4 as a main course.

Some ingredients for white sauces, and home-made grey-green tagliatelle

Four-Flavoured Spaghetti

Time: 30 minutes
Ingredients
450 g (1 lb) spaghetti
1 boned chicken breast
60 g (2 oz) butter
Salt and pepper
75 g (2½ oz) cooked tongue
60 g (2 oz) Gruyère cheese
1 small black truffle (optional)
200 ml (7 fl oz) single cream
100 g (3½ oz) grated Parmesan
　　cheese

Cut the chicken breast into strips and sauté in a knob of butter. When the chicken is golden brown, season with salt and pepper and remove from the pan. Cut the tongue, Gruyère and truffle into fine strips.

Boil the spaghetti in a large saucepanful of salted water. When the pasta is almost cooked, pour a ladleful of the cooking water into a saucepan, add the cream, remaining butter and Parmesan. Heat this sauce over a very low heat without letting it boil.

Preheat the oven to 200°C (400°F, mark 6).

Drain the spaghetti and pour on to a hot serving dish. Pour over the sauce, mix well, season with freshly ground pepper and cover with the strips of chicken, tongue, Gruyère and truffle. Turn the oven off and place the dish inside for a few minutes before serving.

Hint: This white sauce can also be served with egg tagliatelle. Ham may be substituted for the tongue.

Spaghetti 'Buried in Sand'

Time: 20 minutes
Ingredients
450 g (1 lb) spaghetti
Salt and pepper
60 ml (2 fl oz) olive oil
4 tbsp breadcrumbs
1 tbsp chopped parsley
1 red chilli pepper, chopped
2 cloves garlic, chopped

Boil the spaghetti in a large saucepanful of salted water for about 10 minutes.

Meanwhile, pour the oil into a saucepan and heat. Add the breadcrumbs, parsley, chilli pepper and garlic. Season to taste.

Drain the spaghetti, pour into a serving dish and pour over the sauce. Mix well and serve.

Hint: You can complete this dish with a small handful of grated Parmesan cheese if you wish.

'Mimosa' Linguine

Time: 20 minutes
Ingredients
450 g (1 lb) linguine
100 g (3½ oz) ham
200 ml (7 fl oz) single cream
75 g (2½ oz) grated Parmesan cheese
Salt
1 tsp curry powder

Spaghetti 'Buried in Sand'

132

$\frac{1}{2}$ tsp saffron
2 egg yolks, beaten

Chop the ham and heat gently in a saucepan with the cream and cheese.

Meanwhile, boil the linguine in a large saucepanful of salted water. Dissolve the curry powder and the saffron in a bowl with a little of the water the pasta is cooking in, and add to the cream sauce. Mix well, bring to the boil and remove the saucepan from the heat. Add the beaten egg yolks and stir.

Drain the pasta when it is *al dente,* pour over the sauce and serve in a preheated dish.
Hint: Eggs are always added at the last minute, when the pan has been removed from the heat.

Laganelle with Walnut and Pine Nut Sauce

Time: 30 minutes
Ingredients
450 g (1 lb) laganelle (thin dried
    pasta noodles)
30 g (1 oz) pine nuts
150 ml (5 fl oz) olive oil
150 g (5 oz) shelled walnuts
A bunch of fresh parsley, chopped
1 clove garlic, chopped
Salt

Lightly toast the pine nuts in a frying pan with a very small amount of oil. Mix the walnuts and pine nuts and pound them with a pestle in a mortar, or chop them very fine.

Heat 2 tablespoons of the oil in a saucepan and add the chopped parsley and garlic. Sauté for a minute or two and then add the nut mixture. Allow to blend for a minute. Season with salt, remove from the heat and add a few more tablespoons of oil, stirring well.

Boil the laganelle in a large saucepanful of salted water, drain when the pasta is *al dente* and serve with the sauce, adding 3 tablespoons of the water the pasta was cooked in to make it creamier.
Hint: This sauce can also be eaten with potato gnocchi (dumplings) or with lasagne.

Maccheroni with Gruyère

Time: 20 minutes
Ingredients
450 g (1 lb) maccheroni
Salt and pepper
100 g (3$\frac{1}{2}$ oz) grated Gruyère cheese
2 tbsp grated Parmesan cheese
60 g (2 oz) butter

Boil the maccheroni in a large saucepanful of salted water. When the pasta is almost cooked, melt the Gruyère in a bowl with about 175 ml (6 fl oz) of the water the pasta is cooking in, together with the Parmesan and butter. Mix well and sprinkle with pepper.

Laganelle with Walnut and Pine Nut Sauce

Drain the maccheroni and serve with the sauce.

Hint: If you have fontina, Emmenthal or less mature dessert Parmesan, you may substitute them for Gruyère.

Maccheroni with Ricotta

Time: 20 minutes
Ingredients
450 g (1 lb) fluted maccheroni
Salt
200 g (7 oz) ricotta, rubbed through a sieve
A large pinch of nutmeg or cinnamon
1 tsp sugar
30 g (1 oz) butter, cut into small pieces

Boil the maccheroni in a large saucepanful of salted water. Meanwhile, mix the ricotta with a couple of tablespoons of cooking water from the pasta; add the nutmeg or cinnamon and sugar and stir well. Drain the pasta when it is *al dente,* mix in the butter and serve with the ricotta sauce.

Hint: Those on a diet should leave out the butter; the pasta will be just as appetizing.

Farmhouse-Style Penne

Time: 45 minutes
Ingredients
450 g (1 lb) penne
60 g (2 oz) butter
1 small onion, finely chopped
300 g (10 oz) fresh shelled or frozen peas
Salt and pepper
100 g (3½ oz) lean ham, cut into very thin strips
½ stock cube
75 g (2½ oz) Gruyère cheese, cut into small cubes
30 g (1 oz) grated Parmesan cheese

Heat 30 g (1 oz) of the butter in a large saucepan and sauté the onion. Add the peas, salt, pepper and a little water. Simmer gently. In a separate pan, brown the ham in the remaining butter and add to the peas when they are almost cooked. Dissolve the stock cube in 1 or 2 tablespoons of hot water and add to the sauce. Simmer for a few more minutes.

Boil the pasta in a large saucepanful of salted water and drain when it is *al dente.* Pour into the saucepan containing the sauce and turn up the heat for a few seconds, stirring with a wooden spoon. Complete the seasoning with the Gruyère and Parmesan and serve.

Hint: You can also add a few tablespoons of cream to the sauce which will bind it as well as enhancing the flavour.

Farmhouse-Style Penne

Penne with Würstel

Time: 30 minutes
Ingredients
450 g (1 lb) fluted penne
Salt
200 ml (7 fl oz) single cream
Truffle paste (optional)
2 pairs of German Würstel
  sausages, sliced
30 g (1 oz) butter, cut into small
  pieces
60 g (2 oz) grated Parmesan cheese

Boil the penne in a large sauce-panful of salted water. Meanwhile, pour the cream into a saucepan and heat gently. Dissolve the truffle paste in the cream and add the sliced Würstel. Drain the pasta and pour on to a serving dish. Mix in the butter and pour on the sauce, sprinkle with the Parmesan and stir again.

Hint: It is best to dip the Würstel in boiling water for a few seconds to remove their skins before slicing them.

Penne with Salami

Time: 30 minutes
Ingredients
450 g (1 lb) maltagliati (diamond-
  shaped pasta)
150 g (5 oz) salami
30 g (1 oz) butter
3 to 4 tbsp olive oil
A sprig of fresh rosemary
3 tbsp dry white wine
1 whole egg and 1 yolk
Salt and pepper
60 g (2 oz) grated Parmesan cheese

Cut the salami into thin strips and brown in the butter and oil in a saucepan. Put in the rosemary to flavour. When the salami starts to brown, sprinkle with wine and allow to evaporate.

Put the egg and the egg yolk in a large bowl and beat with a few pinches of salt, pepper and the grated cheese. Whisk well to bind the ingredients together.

Boil the pasta in a large sauce-panful of salted water and drain when the penne are *al dente*. Pour the pasta into the dish containing the egg mixture and stir quickly to 'cook' the egg mixture with the hot pasta. Then add the salami and the pan juices, removing the rosemary. Mix again and serve at once.

Hint: To complete the meal, serve a main course of steak and a mixed salad of fennel, chicory, carrot and celery with a vinaigrette dressing.

Rigatoni 'In the Pink'

Time: 45 minutes
Ingredients
450 g (1 lb) rigatoni (large fluted
  dried pasta tubes)
½ onion, sliced
30 g (1 oz) butter
2 tbsp olive oil

Penne with Salami

138

60 g (2 oz) lean bacon, diced
200 g (7 oz) peeled tomatoes
Salt
$\frac{1}{4}$ tsp sugar
150 ml (5 fl oz) single cream

Fry the onion in the butter and oil until it softens but does not brown. Then add the bacon and brown well before adding the tomatoes. Simmer for about 20 minutes, stirring frequently. Add a little salt and sugar to bring out the flavour of the tomatoes. Finally, add the cream and stir until the sauce has a creamy texture.

Preheat the oven to 180°C (350°F, mark 4).

Boil the rigatoni in a large saucepanful of salted water and drain when the pasta is *al dente*. Pour into an ovenproof dish and pour over the sauce. Bake in the oven for about 10 minutes.

Hint: As a main course, or as a one-course meal accompanied by the rigatoni, serve veal escalopes lightly floured and salted, fried in butter and oil and sprinkled with a little dry Marsala.

Rigatoni with Marrow

Time: 1 hour
Ingredients
450 g (1 lb) rigatoni or large zite (large fluted or smooth dried pasta tubes)
800 g (1$\frac{3}{4}$ lb) vegetable marrow
75 g (2$\frac{1}{2}$ oz) butter
Salt
A few pinches of nutmeg
60 g (2 oz) grated Parmesan cheese

Peel and dice the marrow. Melt 60 g (2 oz) of the butter and add the diced marrow, simmering gently and stirring frequently.

Boil the rigatoni, or the zite cut into 8 cm (3 in) lengths, in a large saucepanful of salted water. Drain when the pasta is *al dente* and cut the remaining butter into slivers to mix in with the pasta. Add the marrow and its cooking juices, some grated nutmeg and the cheese and mix again. Serve at once.

Hint: Reserve a few tablespoons of water from cooking the pasta and add it to the pasta just before mixing in the sauce (or add a few tablespoons of hot cream).

Rigatoni with Marrow

Spicy Farfalloni with Walnuts

Time: 20 minutes
Ingredients
450 g (1 lb) farfalloni (large dried
  pasta butterflies)
Salt
60 g (2 oz) butter
10 walnuts, coarsely chopped
100 g (3½ oz) ham, diced
1 tsp white peppercorns, crushed in
  a mortar or with the handle of a
  knife

Boil the farfalloni in a large saucepanful of salted water and drain when the pasta is *al dente*. Set aside a ladleful of the water the pasta was cooked in.

In a small pan, melt the butter in the pasta water and add the walnuts, ham and pepper. Season the pasta with the sauce and serve.
Hint: A little coarsely grated dessert Parmesan (that is, still soft, medium mature Parmesan) may be added to the sauce. Use a carrot grater.

Conchiglie with Creamy Cheese Sauce

Time: 25 minutes
Ingredients
450 g (1 lb) conchiglie
Salt
100 g (3½ oz) Gorgonzola cheese, cut
  into small pieces
100 g (3½ oz) crescenza cheese, cut
  into small pieces
4 to 5 tbsp milk
75 g (2½ oz) butter, cut into slivers
60 g (2 oz) grated Parmesan cheese

Boil the conchiglie in a large saucepanful of salted water.

Melt the Gorgonzola and the crescenza by heating them very gently in a saucepan with the milk. Stir constantly with a wooden spoon.

Warm a serving dish by pouring boiling water into it and then drying it. Drain the pasta when it is *al dente* and pour into the dish. Mix in the butter at once and, as soon as it has melted, pour over the sauce. Sprinkle with the Parmesan and serve immediately.
Hint: If you wish, you can add some freshly ground white pepper at the last minute.

Truffled Sedanini

Time: 30 minutes
Ingredients
450 g (1 lb) sedanini (small fluted
  curved maccheroni)
Salt and white pepper
60 g (2 oz) butter, cut into slivers
2 tbsp single cream
100 g (3½ oz) grated Parmesan
  cheese
1 small white truffle (optional), cut
  into very thin slices

Boil the sedanini in a large saucepanful of salted water. Drain

142

when the pasta is just *al dente* and run under the cold tap for a second to stop the cooking.

Preheat the oven to 200°C (400°F, mark 6).

Transfer the pasta to an oven-proof dish and mix in the butter at once. Mix the cream and the cheese together and pour over the pasta. Scatter the truffle slices over the top and sprinkle liberally with pepper. Place in the oven for about 10 minutes.

Hint: To obtain the full pungency from pepper, keep peppercorns in a pepper-mill and grind them at the last minute. White pepper is usually preferable with white sauces.

Sedanini in Crab Sauce

Time: 1¼ hours
Ingredients
450 g (1 lb) sedanini (small fluted
   curved maccheroni)
1 fresh crab or 1 tin of crab meat
A little dry white wine
1 bay leaf
1 carrot
1 stick celery
200 ml (7 fl oz) single cream
60 g (2 oz) butter
A pinch of paprika
Salt

Wash the crab and boil it in a *court-bouillon* of water to cover with the dry white wine, bay leaf, carrot and celery. Allow 10 to 15 minutes per 450 g (1 lb). Drain, allow to cool and remove the meat from the shell. Cut half of the meat into small pieces and liquidize the other half with a little of the cream. If you are using tinned crab, drain and continue as for fresh crab.

Melt the butter (reserving a knob) in a saucepan and add the puréed crab, the rest of the cream and the paprika and leave on a low heat to allow the flavours to blend.

Meanwhile, boil the sedanini in a large saucepanful of salted water, drain when the pasta is *al dente* and place in a preheated serving dish. Pour over the hot crab sauce. Sauté the rest of the crab briefly in the remaining butter for a garnish.

Hint: It is sometimes difficult to find fresh crabs in the shops which is why you may have to resort to tinned crab, which is almost as delicate.

Superlative Pappardelle

Time: 1½ hours
Ingredients
450 g (1 lb) fresh or dried pappardelle
   or wide noodles
4 artichokes
1 lemon
1 small onion, finely chopped
100 g (3½ oz) butter
Salt and pepper

1 tsp beef extract
A little stock
100 g (3½ oz) turkey leg meat, cut
 into thin strips
3 tbsp Madeira
200 ml (7 fl oz) single cream
60 g (2 oz) grated Parmesan cheese
100 g (3½ oz) ham, cut into thin
 strips

Clean the artichokes and remove the tips and the hard outer leaves. Slice the hearts and immediately immerse them in water and lemon juice to prevent them from turning black. Sauté the onion in 30 g (1 oz) of the butter, add the sliced artichokes, salt and pepper and simmer over a low heat. Dissolve ½ tsp beef extract in a little stock and add to the pan.

In a separate pan, brown the turkey meat in 15 g (½ oz) of the butter and then pour in the Madeira. When the Madeira has evaporated, dissolve the rest of the beef extract in a tablespoon of boiling water and add to the turkey.

Boil the pappardelle in a large saucepanful of salted water. While the pasta is cooking, pre-heat the oven to 200°C (400°F, mark 6).

Drain the pasta when it is just *al dente*. Melt the remaining butter in the saucepan the pasta was cooked in and return the pappardelle to the pan. Mix the cream in carefully, add pepper and continue cooking gently on top of the stove. Remove from the heat and mix in about half of the cheese. Spread the pasta in an even layer in the base of an oven-proof dish then cover with a layer of ham, a layer of pasta, then the artichokes and their sauce and another layer of pasta. Finish with a layer of turkey with its sauce. Sprinkle over the remaining cheese and put in the oven for a few minutes.

Hint: You can vary this dish by substituting chicken for the turkey and Marsala for the Madeira.

Tagliatelle with Triple Butter Sauce

Time: 10 minutes
Ingredients
450 g (1 lb) fresh or dried tagliatelle
Salt
150 g (5 oz) butter, cut into slivers
150 g (5 oz) grated dessert Parmesan
 cheese

Ten minutes before you are ready to eat, boil the tagliatelle in a large saucepanful of salted water. Drain when the pasta is *al dente*. Heat a serving dish by pouring boiling water into it and then drying it. Pour in the pasta. Carefully mix in the butter and cheese and serve at once.

Tagliatelle with Triple Butter Sauce

Hint: As this rich buttery dish is very high in calories it is advisable to eat only raw or cooked vegetables with little butter or oil for the other meals that day!

Fettuccine with Truffle

Time: 20 minutes
Ingredients
450 g (1 lb) fresh or dried fettuccine
Salt and white pepper
60 g (2 oz) butter
60 g (2 oz) grated Parmesan cheese
1 white truffle (optional), thinly
 sliced

Boil the fettuccine in a large saucepanful of slightly salted water and drain when the pasta is *al dente*. Heat a serving dish by pouring boiling water into it and then drying it thoroughly. Melt the butter in a small saucepan. Pour the pasta into the serving dish and pour over the butter and half the cheese. Add freshly ground pepper and mix carefully. Arrange the slices of truffle on top and serve with the rest of the cheese.

Hint: If you like, you can serve this dish with a hot meat sauce in a separate sauceboat.

Fettuccine with Truffle

STUFFED PASTA

Stuffed pasta means fresh egg pasta with meat or vegetable fillings. The shapes and stuffings vary from one region to another. In Emilia-Romagna, for example, you find the famous tortellini, cappelletti and ravioli; in Piedmont, agnolotti; and in Friuli-Venezia Giulia, ofelle, and so on. They all make substantial first courses.

Meat fillings are prepared from various ingredients—minced beef, veal, pork, sausage-meat, giblets, smoked or cooked ham or mortadella—enriched with cheese and egg to bind the ingredients together. Non-meat fillings are made with various vegetables —chard, spinach or other greens, marrow or potatoes—sometimes mixed with ricotta or with other cheeses and spices.

Each type of stuffing requires a particular sauce for the combination of flavours to be appetizing. As a general rule, pasta with meat filling needs a rich meat ragù while pasta with vegetable stuffing is best with delicate sauces made from butter, cream and various kinds of cheese.

There are also sauces based on mushrooms, nuts and herbs which are suited to one or other of the kinds of stuffed pasta.

A larger type of stuffed pasta are cannelloni—little rolls of fresh pasta (either yellow or green) stuffed with meat or vegetables.

Cannelloni can be served with tomato sauce or with meat ragù and are usually topped with béchamel sauce. While the types of pasta already mentioned come from the north of Italy, cannelloni, in various forms, are also to be found in the centre and south of Italy.

And finally, there is the rotolo—a sort of giant cannellone, made from egg pasta with a non-meat stuffing. It can be served with butter and cheese, or with a stew, or simply with tomatoes and basil. Cannelloni and rotolo usually constitute a main course.

The recipes that follow will serve 6 as a first course or 4 as a main course.

Home-made stuffed cappelletti and commercial dried cannelloni for filling

149

Tasty Agnolotti

Time: 2 hours
Ingredients
For the pasta:
400 g (14 oz) white or strong flour
2 eggs
A little water
Salt
For the filling:
100 g (3½ oz) calf's brain
60 g (2 oz) fresh spicy sausage
225 g (8 oz) braised beef
100 g (3½ oz) roast pork
300 g (10 oz) spinach, cabbage or
    endive
30 g (1 oz) butter
3 tbsp grated Parmesan cheese
Salt and pepper
A little nutmeg
1 egg
Meat stock (with the fat skimmed off)
For the sauce:
75 g (2½ oz) butter
75 g (2½ oz) grated Parmesan cheese
175 ml (6 fl oz) home-made tomato
    sauce

First, prepare the filling: scald the brain in boiling water for a few seconds and sauté the sausage in a frying pan over a high heat. Mince together with the beef and pork. Boil the spinach and wring it thoroughly. Chop and sauté in the butter then add to the meat mixture. Add the Parmesan and season with salt, pepper and nutmeg. Bind all the ingredients with the egg; you should obtain a soft but firm paste.

Prepare the egg pasta with the ingredients listed, and by the method described on page 21. Make agnolotti following the instructions on page 34 and fill them with the meat mixture.

Boil the agnolotti in a large saucepanful of meat stock and drain when the pasta is *al dente*. Put into a dish and pour over alternate layers of melted butter and cheese. Serve with the tomato sauce.

Hint: It is best to make agnolotti when you have time to spend as long as is necessary in the kitchen; it takes a lot of patience to make the dough, and the meats require slow and attentive cooking.

Ravioli with Melted Butter

Time: 1¾ hours
Ingredients
For the pasta:
400 g (14 oz) white or strong flour
4 eggs
Salt
For the filling:
1 small onion, chopped
60 g (2 oz) smoked ham, chopped
30 g (1 oz) butter
2 tbsp olive oil
300 g (10 oz) minced veal
100 g (3½ oz) fresh spicy sausage
A little dry white wine
1 tsp beef extract
Salt and pepper
30 g (1 oz) grated Parmesan cheese
1 egg
A little nutmeg

Tasty Agnolotti

For the sauce:
75 g (2½ oz) butter
A sprig of fresh sage
75 g (2½ oz) grated Parmesan cheese

First, prepare the filling: sauté the onion and the ham in the butter and oil. Add the veal and sausage and brown. Pour over the wine and let it evaporate. Dilute the beef extract in a little hot water and add to the other ingredients. Season with salt and pepper and simmer until a dry mixture is obtained. Remove from the heat and stir in the Parmesan and the egg. Season with nutmeg.

Prepare the egg pasta with the ingredients listed, following the instructions on page 21.

Make ravioli as described on page 40, and fill with the stuffing. Boil the ravioli in a large saucepanful of salted water, drain and place in a dish. Heat the butter with the sage until it is hazelnut-coloured. Remove the sage and pour the butter over the ravioli, alternately with the cheese.

Hint: Leftover braised or roast meat can be added to the stuffing.

Ravioli Stuffed with Spinach and Ricotta

Time: 1½ hours
Ingredients
For the pasta:
400 g (14 oz) white or strong flour

4 eggs
Salt
For the filling:
1 kg (2¼ lb) spinach or greens
Salt
1 tbsp chopped parsley
75 g (2½ oz) grated Parmesan cheese
200 g (7 oz) ricotta
1 egg
A little nutmeg
For the sauce:
100 g (3½ oz) butter
Salt
75 g (2½ oz) grated Parmesan cheese

First, prepare the filling: remove the stalks and wash the spinach thoroughly. Heat in a frying pan without adding any more water (the water remaining on the leaves will be sufficient). Add salt and simmer in the uncovered pan. Drain and wring in a clean tea-towel. Leave to cool, then chop and put into a bowl. Add the parsley, Parmesan, ricotta, egg and nutmeg and mix.

Prepare the egg pasta following the instructions on page 21 and make ravioli as described on page 40. Fill with the stuffing. Boil the ravioli in a large saucepanful of salted water over a medium heat in an uncovered saucepan. Meanwhile, melt the butter with a pinch of salt.

As the ravioli gradually float to the surface, drain them with a slotted spoon and season them with the melted butter and Par-

Ravioli Stuffed with Spinach and Ricotta

mesan cheese in alternate layers.
Hint: Do not drain the ravioli in a colander as with other types of pasta; the ravioli may stick and break and the filling will be lost.

Cappelletti with Mushroom Sauce

Time: $1\frac{3}{4}$ hours
Ingredients
For the pasta:
400 g (14 oz) white or strong flour
4 eggs
Salt
For the filling:
30 g (1 oz) butter
1 tbsp olive oil
225 g (8 oz) turkey or chicken meat, cut into fine strips
60 g (2 oz) smoked ham, cut into fine strips
1 slice of mortadella, cut into fine strips
Salt and pepper
2 fresh sage leaves
2 chicken livers, gall removed
2 tbsp Marsala
100 g ($3\frac{1}{2}$ oz) ricotta
75 g ($2\frac{1}{2}$ oz) grated Parmesan cheese
2 tbsp breadcrumbs
1 egg
A little nutmeg
For the sauce:
30 g (1 oz) dried cep mushrooms
60 g (2 oz) butter
1 clove garlic
A little dry white wine
Salt and pepper
$\frac{1}{4}$ tsp beef extract
200 ml (7 fl oz) single cream
A bunch of fresh parsley, chopped
4 tbsp grated Parmesan cheese

First, prepare the filling: melt the butter with 1 tablespoon of oil and add the meat, the ham and the mortadella. Season with salt and pepper and add the sage. Brown and then add the chicken livers. Pour over 2 tablespoons of Marsala and allow to evaporate.

Remove the pan from the heat and take out the sage leaves. Chop the mixture, preferably in a meat mincer, and collect it in a bowl. Add the ricotta, the Parmesan, the breadcrumbs, the egg and some grated nutmeg and mix well to obtain a smooth paste. Taste and add salt if necessary.

Prepare the egg pasta with the ingredients listed, following the instructions on page 21. Make cappelletti as described on page 42 and stuff with the filling.

While they are drying, prepare the sauce: soften the mushrooms in warm water. Slice them and brown them in the butter with the whole clove of garlic. Pour in the wine and allow it to evaporate. Add salt, pepper and the beef extract and simmer for a few minutes. Add the cream, bring to the boil and sprinkle with parsley just before removing the pan from the heat.

Cappelletti with Mushroom Sauce

Boil the cappelletti in a large saucepanful of salted water. Drain and pour over alternate layers of mushroom sauce and Parmesan, or finish the pasta with butter and serve the sauce separately.

Hint: Use fresh cep mushrooms when in season. Do not wash them: it is sufficient to cut off the bottom of the stalk and wipe the top with a damp cloth.

Cappelletti with Bolognese Sauce

Time: 2¼ hours
Ingredients
For the pasta:
400 g (14 oz) white or strong flour
4 eggs
Salt
For the filling:
1 small onion, chopped
100 g (3½ oz) smoked ham, chopped
2 tbsp olive oil
30 g (1 oz) butter
1 carrot, chopped
1 stick celery, chopped
1 bay leaf
2 juniper berries
225 g (8 oz) lean minced beef
Salt and pepper
60 ml (2 fl oz) red wine
100 ml (3 fl oz) dry white wine
½ tbsp concentrated tomato purée, dissolved in a little water
100 g (3½ oz) fresh sausage
2 to 3 tbsp grated Parmesan cheese
A little nutmeg
1 egg
2 to 3 tbsp breadcrumbs

For the sauce:
20 g (⅔ oz) dried mushrooms
½ onion, chopped
½ carrot, chopped
½ stick celery, chopped
30 g (1 oz) bacon fat, chopped
20 g (⅔ oz) butter
200 g (7 oz) minced beef
100 ml (3 fl oz) dry white wine
2 to 3 tbsp concentrated tomato purée, dissolved in a ladleful of hot water
2 chicken livers, finely chopped
Salt and pepper
A little nutmeg
60 g (1 oz) grated Parmesan cheese

Prepare the filling first: sauté the onion and ham in the oil and butter, add the carrot, celery, bay leaf and juniper berries and brown. Then add the minced beef, salt and pepper and brown thoroughly. Pour in the wine and allow to evaporate. Add the tomato purée and continue simmering. Add the sausage towards the end.

Remove the bay leaf and juniper berries. The sauce should be thick by now. Add the Parmesan and a little grated nutmeg, the egg and the breadcrumbs and mix well to obtain a smooth paste. Taste and add salt if necessary.

Make the egg pasta with the ingredients listed, following the instructions on page 21. Prepare cappelletti as described on page 42 and stuff with the filling.

While they are drying, prepare the sauce. Soak the mushrooms in warm water. Fry the onion, carrot, celery and bacon fat in the butter. Brown the meat, pour in the wine and allow to evaporate. Add the tomato purée, then drain and slice the mushrooms and add these too, together with the chicken livers. Season with salt, pepper and nutmeg and simmer for about 1 hour.

Boil the cappelletti in a large saucepanful of salted water and drain when the pasta is *al dente*. Serve with alternate layers of sauce and Parmesan.

Hint: This is the classic Bolognese ragù, which is extremely substantial. A large helping constitutes a complete meal.

Cappelletti Pie

Time: 3 hours
Ingredients
450 g (1 lb) cappelletti, prepared according to the instructions on page 42
Salt
A knob of butter
A few tbsp breadcrumbs
75 g (2½ oz) grated Parmesan cheese
1 egg
For the pastry:
300 g (10 oz) white flour
Salt
100 g (3½ oz) butter
30 g (1 oz) sugar
3 egg yolks

For the ragù:
75 g (2½ oz) butter
60 g (2 oz) bacon, chopped
1 onion, chopped
1 carrot, chopped
1 stick celery, chopped
150 g (5 oz) lonza (cured fillet of pork sausage), minced
150 g (5 oz) lean minced beef
500 g (1 lb 2 oz) ripe tomatoes, peeled and rubbed through a sieve or 1 225 g (8 oz) tin of peeled tomatoes
1 clove
1 bay leaf
Salt and pepper
100 ml (3 fl oz) single cream
2 to 3 chicken livers, finely diced
For the béchamel:
40 g (1½ oz) butter
2 tbsp flour
½ litre (18 fl oz) milk, heated
Salt and pepper
A little nutmeg

First, prepare the ragù: heat half of the butter and sauté the bacon, onion, carrot and celery. Add the minced meats and brown. Add the tomatoes, clove, bay leaf, a pinch of salt and pepper and simmer for about 1 hour, adding a little cream from time to time. Add the chicken livers a few minutes before the sauce is cooked.

While the ragù is simmering, prepare the sweet shortcrust pastry: pour the flour on to a pastry board in a heap and make a well in the centre. Put in a pinch of salt, the butter, the sugar and 3 egg yolks. Mix vigorously to incorporate the flour into the eggs and butter. When you have a smooth dough (knead it as little as possible with your hands), wrap it in clingfilm and put it in the lowest part of the fridge.

Meanwhile, make a béchamel sauce with the butter, flour and milk. Season with salt, pepper and nutmeg. Bring to the boil and remove from the heat.

Preheat the oven to 180°C (350°F, mark 4).

Boil the cappelletti in a large saucepanful of salted water, drain when the pasta is *al dente* and pour over some of the ragù. Divide the pastry into two pieces, one twice the size of the other. Roll out the larger piece into a round 3 mm ($\frac{1}{8}$ in) thick. Butter a circular pie dish and sprinkle with breadcrumbs. Line the dish with the larger piece of dough. Pour in the cappelletti, alternating them with ragù, béchamel and grated Parmesan. Cover with the other piece of pastry cut into a round the same diameter as the pie dish. Cut off any extra pastry and seal the pie with the prongs of a fork all round the edge. Make a small hole in the centre and insert a piece of rolled paper to enable the steam to escape during cooking. Then beat the whole egg

and brush the pastry with it.

Place the pie in the oven for about 1 hour. Remove from the oven and leave it to 'rest' for a few minutes before serving.

Hint: If you do not like the combination of sweet and savoury, you can use plain shortcrust pastry instead; you can, of course, buy it ready-made and frozen.

Marrow Tortelli

Time: 2$\frac{1}{2}$ hours
Ingredients
For the pasta:
400 g (14 oz) white or strong flour
4 eggs
Salt
For the filling and the sauce:
2 kg (4$\frac{1}{2}$ lb) firm vegetable marrow
100 g (3$\frac{1}{2}$ oz) ground almonds
100 g (3$\frac{1}{2}$ oz) grated Parmesan
    cheese
1 lemon
60 g (1 oz) candied citron peel, finely
    chopped
A little nutmeg
1 egg
Salt and pepper
Breadcrumbs (optional)
60 g (1 oz) butter
2 tbsp olive oil
A sprig of fresh sage

First, prepare the filling: slice the marrow and remove the seeds, then bake in the oven. Scoop out the soft flesh with a large spoon and throw away the peel. Rub the marrow through a sieve and add the ground almonds, half the Parmesan, the grated rind of the lemon (grate only the yellow rind not the white pith), the candied peel, nutmeg, the egg and a pinch of salt and pepper. Mix thoroughly with a wooden spoon. If the mixture is too soft, add a small quantity of breadcrumbs.

Make the egg pasta with the ingredients listed, following the instructions on page 21. Make half-moon-shaped tortelli and fill them with the marrow stuffing.

Boil the tortelli in a large saucepanful of salted water until *al dente*. Meanwhile, heat the butter and oil with the sage. Drain the tortelli into a tureen, pouring over alternate layers of the butter sauce (discard the sage) and the rest of the Parmesan.

Hint: To give the tortelli a pleasing shape, cut them out with a round, serrated pastry cutter, making the circles about 5 cm (2 in) in diameter.

Casonsei Brescia-Style

Time: 1½ hours
Ingredients
For the pasta:
400 g (14 oz) white or strong flour
4 eggs
Salt
For the filling:
The soft crumb of 1 bread roll, crust discarded
A little milk
300 g (10 oz) sausage-meat, crumbled into small pieces
100 g (3½ oz) grated Parmesan cheese
Salt and pepper
For the sauce:
100 g (3½ oz) butter
A few fresh sage leaves
Pepper
100 g (3½ oz) grated Parmesan cheese

First, prepare the filling: soak the bread in a little milk. Squeeze it out by hand and put into a bowl with the sausage-meat, cheese and salt and pepper if you wish. Mix well.

Prepare the egg pasta with the ingredients listed, following the instructions on page 21. Make large ravioli in the shape of calzoncini (half-moon shapes), as described on page 36, and fill with the stuffing.

Boil the casonsei in a large saucepanful of salted water. While the pasta is cooking, melt the butter with the sage and a pinch of pepper. Drain the casonsei with a slotted spoon and serve with the sage-flavoured butter and Parmesan.

Hint: Wait a few minutes before serving the casonsei to allow the pasta to absorb fully the flavour of the sauce, and the cheese to melt.

Casonsei with Pumpkin and Pheasant

Time: 2¼ hours
Ingredients
For the pasta:
400 g (14 oz) white flour
4 eggs
Salt
For the filling:
700 g (1½ lb) pumpkin, seeded and
　peeled
60 g (2 oz) grated Parmesan cheese
200 g (7 oz) ricotta
Salt and pepper
1 egg
*For the sauce and to season the
　casonsei:*
1 pheasant weighing about 600 g
　(1¼ lb), dressed
100 g (3½ oz) sliced bacon
Salt
Peppercorns
A few fresh sage leaves
30 g (1 oz) butter
A few tbsp olive oil
30 g (1 oz) grated smoked ricotta or
　grated Parmesan cheese

First, prepare the stuffing for the casonsei: bake the pumpkin (or, if you don't have the time, boil it) and rub it through a sieve. Collect the purée in a bowl and add the Parmesan, the ricotta, salt, pepper and the egg. Mix well.

Prepare the egg pasta with the ingredients listed, following the instructions on page 21. Make large calzoncini as described on page 36. Fill them with the pumpkin mixture.

Preheat the oven to 220°C (425°F, mark 7).

Chop the pheasant's liver and gizzard (if you have them) together with half the bacon, salt, a few peppercorns and the sage. Stuff the pheasant with the mixture and truss the bird. Butter a flameproof, ovenproof dish and sprinkle with oil. Place the bird in the dish and cover with the remaining bacon. Roast in the oven for about 1 hour. When it is cooked, remove all the meat and cut it into tiny pieces. Scoop out the stuffing.

Skim the fat off the juices which will have collected in the dish the bird was cooked in and add the crumbled stuffing and the pheasant meat; heat for 1 minute.

Ten minutes before you are ready to serve, boil the casonsei in a large saucepanful of salted water. Drain, a few at a time, with a slotted spoon, and arrange in a tureen. Alternate with layers of the pheasant sauce. To complete, sprinkle the grated smoked ricotta over the top.

Hint: This typical dish from Lombardy can be served as a main course. It is possible to use Parmesan instead of ricotta.

Marubini with Financière Sauce

Time: 1½ hours
Ingredients
For the pasta:
400 g (14 oz) white flour
4 eggs
Salt
For the filling:
200 g (7 oz) braised or roast beef,
   chopped
100 g (3½ oz) roast veal, chopped
100 g (3½ oz) boiled calf's brain,
   chopped
75 g (2½ oz) grated Parmesan cheese
Salt and pepper
A little nutmeg
1 to 2 eggs
For the ragù:
40 g (1½ oz) butter
½ carrot, chopped
½ onion, chopped
½ stick celery, chopped
3 chicken gizzards and 4 chicken
   livers, cleaned and coarsely
   chopped
30 g (1 oz) dried mushrooms,
   soaked, drained and sliced
60 ml (2 fl oz) dry white wine
A little stock, heated
Salt
1 tsp flour

First, prepare the filling: mix the chopped beef, veal and brain in a bowl and add the Parmesan, salt, pepper, nutmeg and an egg to bind the ingredients together. You may find you need 2 eggs. You should obtain a soft but dry mixture.

Now, prepare the ragù: melt the butter in a pan over a moderate heat and sauté the carrot, onion and celery. Add the gizzards and, when they are almost cooked, the livers and mushrooms. Brown for a few minutes then pour the wine over the giblets. When the wine has evaporated, pour in a little hot stock. Add salt, cover and simmer for about 30 minutes. When cooked, add a knob of butter mixed with the flour to thicken the ragù.

Prepare the egg pasta with the ingredients listed, following the instructions on page 21. Make marubini as described on page 36 and stuff with the filling.

Boil the marubini in a large saucepanful of salted water or stock, drain and serve with the ragù.

Hint: If the stuffing mixture is too firm, add more egg, or, if it is too moist, add breadcrumbs. The traditional regional recipe suggests cooking the marubini in a good meat broth, but they are just as tasty boiled in water and drained—in which case, they can be made a little bigger.

Ofelle Trieste-Style

Time: 2 hours
Ingredients
For the pasta:
1 kg (2¼ lb) floury potatoes
Salt
200 g (7 oz) white flour
1 egg
1 tsp dried yeast
For the filling:
800 g (1¾ lb) spinach or greens
100 g (3½ oz) pure pork sausage,
   chopped
150 g (5 oz) minced veal
Salt
30 g (1 oz) butter
1 onion, chopped
1 tbsp chopped parsley
1 clove garlic, chopped
For the sauce:
100 g (3½ oz) fresh butter
100 g (3½ oz) grated Parmesan
   cheese

First, prepare the filling: wash the spinach (or greens), drain, boil in a little water, drain well, chop and put into a bowl with the sausage, veal and salt. Heat the butter and sauté the onion, then add the contents of the bowl. Simmer for a few minutes. Add the parsley and garlic, sauté briefly and remove from the heat. Leave to cool.

Now make the pasta: boil the potatoes in salted water, peel and purée them. Put the purée on the pastry board, add the flour, egg, salt and yeast and mix to a dough similar to that for potato gnocchi but a bit firmer.

Roll out the dough and make large ravioli (see page 36) and fill with the stuffing. Boil in a large saucepanful of salted water, drain and serve with melted butter and Parmesan.

Hint: The dough will seem rather moist because it is prepared from potatoes. Use a long spatula to ease it off the pastry board from time to time.

Panciuti 'al Preboggion'

Time: 2 hours
Ingredients
For the pasta:
400 g (14 oz) white or strong flour
A little dry white wine
Salt
For the filling:
600 g (1¼ lb) greens
200 g (7 oz) borage
500 g (1 lb 2 oz) mixed herbs and
   greens such as chard, cabbage
   leaves, wild chicory, chervil or
   vine leaves
1 clove garlic, finely chopped
2 eggs
75 g (2½ oz) grated Parmesan cheese
150 g (5 oz) ricotta
Salt and pepper
For the sauce:
150 g (5 oz) walnuts, blanched and
   peeled
A handful of soft bread, without
   crust, soaked in water and
   thoroughly squeezed out
30 g (1 oz) pine nuts (optional)
Salt
1 clove garlic

Panciuti 'al Preboggion'

162

Curdled milk (substitute full-cream
 milk or single cream)
 3 to 4 tbsp olive oil

First, prepare the filling: wash the greens, borage and herbs and boil in a little water. Drain well, chop finely and put in a bowl. Add the garlic, eggs, Parmesan, ricotta, salt and pepper and mix.

Prepare the pasta with the ingredients listed, following the instructions on page 21. Cut the dough into large rounds, or triangles if you prefer, and make triangular or half-moon-shaped ravioli as described on page 36. Fill with the stuffing.

Before cooking the panciuti prepare the sauce: put the walnuts, bread, pine nuts, a few pinches of salt and the garlic into a mortar or liquidizer and blend to a paste. Rub this paste through a sieve and dilute with the curdled milk (milk or cream) to obtain a thickish sauce. Stir in the olive oil.

Boil the ravioli in a large saucepanful of salted water, drain and serve with the walnut sauce.

Hint: 'Preboggion' is a mixture of herbs that grow wild in the Ligurian hills where this dish originated. If you prefer, instead of the herbs and greens suggested in the list of ingredients, you may use simply greens and flavour the mixture with chopped parsley and garlic.

Pasta Piena with Cheese Sauce

Time: 1½ hours
Ingredients
For the pasta:
400 g (14 oz) white or strong flour
4 eggs
Salt
For the filling:
200 g (7 oz) beef marrow
100 g (3½ oz) ham, finely chopped
12 tbsp grated Parmesan cheese
4 eggs
Salt and pepper
A little nutmeg
A few tbsp breadcrumbs
For the sauce:
100 g (3½ oz) butter
250 ml (9 fl oz) single cream
Salt and pepper
100 g (3½ oz) Gruyère cheese, grated

First, prepare the filling: blanch the beef marrow in boiling water and rub it through a sieve into a bowl with the ham, Parmesan, the eggs, a pinch of pepper, salt, nutmeg and breadcrumbs (enough to obtain a fairly soft mixture). Mix with a wooden spoon to obtain a smooth paste.

Prepare the egg pasta with the ingredients listed, following the instructions on page 21. Shape the pasta as described on page 40 and fill with the stuffing.

Boil the filled pasta in a large saucepanful of salted water or stock until *al dente*. Meanwhile, prepare the sauce: melt the butter in a large pan, add the cream and allow it to reduce and thicken a little. Add salt and pepper and then the Gruyère. Stir over a moderate heat until the cheese has melted.

Drain the pasta and pour into the pan with the sauce. Stir carefully for a few seconds and serve while the sauce is still 'gooey'.

Hint: You can add Gorgonzola cheese to the sauce if you prefer a more pungent flavour. According to the regional recipe, the pasta is cooked in stock, but it is also excellent when boiled in water as described here.

Cannelloni with Mascherpone

Time: 1½ hours
Ingredients
450 g (1 lb) home-made or packet lasagne
400 g (14 oz) greens (spinach, cabbage, chard)
200 g (7 oz) ricotta
100 g (3½ oz) mascherpone cheese
Salt and pepper
60 g (2 oz) butter
30 g (1 oz) flour
200 ml (7 fl oz) milk
100 ml (3 fl oz) single cream
150 g (5 oz) fontina cheese, half grated, half cubed

Boil the greens, chop and mix them with the ricotta, mascherpone and salt and pepper.

Melt 30 g (1 oz) of the butter and incorporate the flour. Heat the milk and add it gradually, stirring continuously. Simmer for a few minutes and stir in the cream. Bring to the boil, stirring all the time, add the grated fontina and remove from the heat.

Preheat the oven to 200°C (400°F, mark 6).

Boil the lasagne in a large saucepanful of salted water, drain when the pasta is *al dente* and lay it on a clean tea-towel. Put a little of the cheese and vegetable mixture in the centre of each rectangle, roll the lasagne up and arrange the cannelloni in a large buttered ovenproof dish. Cover with the sauce. Scatter over the cubes of fontina and top with slivers of butter. Bake in the oven for about 15 minutes.

Hint: To make a lighter dish, omit the mascherpone and increase the amount of ricotta, which must be very fresh and soft.

Cannelloni Filled with Chicken

Time: 1¾ hours
Ingredients
450 g (1 lb) home-made or packet lasagne
For the filling:
2 tbsp olive oil
20 g (⅔ oz) butter
½ spring chicken, washed and dried

Salt and pepper
1 lemon, squeezed
100 g (3½ oz) smoked ham
60 g (2 oz) grated Parmesan cheese
2 eggs
For the sauce:
2 tbsp olive oil
60 g (2 oz) butter
1 small onion, chopped
1 225 g (8 oz) tin of peeled tomatoes,
    rubbed through a sieve
Salt
60 g (2 oz) grated Parmesan cheese

First, prepare the filling: heat the oil and the butter and brown the chicken. Add salt and pepper and the juice from the lemon. Cook the chicken, turning it often. Drain, discard the skin, remove all the meat and put it through a mincer with the ham. Mix in the Parmesan, eggs, a pinch of salt and some of the cooking juices from the chicken.

Now make the tomato sauce: heat the oil and 20 g (⅔ oz) of the butter and soften the onion, then add the tomatoes and salt. Simmer until the sauce thickens.

Preheat the oven to 200°C (400°F, mark 6).

Boil the lasagne, a few at a time, in a large saucepanful of salted water, drain when the pasta is *al dente* and lay the lasagne on a clean tea-towel. Place a little stuffing in the centre of each rectangle and roll up the cannelloni. Arrange them in layers in a buttered ovenproof dish, pouring a little tomato sauce over each layer. Sprinkle the cheese and slivers of the remaining butter over the top. Place in the oven for about 15 minutes.

Hint: This light, chicken-based filling is particularly recommended for children, and is also delicious served with a sauce made with fresh mushrooms.

Cannelloni Simona

Time: 2 hours
Ingredients
450 g (1 lb) home-made or packet
    lasagne
Salt
30 g (1 oz) butter
100 g (3½ oz) smoked ham, thinly
    sliced
For the filling:
20 g (⅔ oz) butter
A little olive oil
225 g (8 oz) minced pork
225 g (8 oz) chicken breast
1 stock cube
A little dry white wine
100 g (3½ oz) grated Parmesan
    cheese
A little nutmeg
Salt and pepper
1 egg
For the sauce:
1 onion, chopped
20 g (⅔ oz) butter
2 tbsp olive oil
60 g (2 oz) dried mushrooms, soaked
    in warm water, drained and
    coarsely chopped

2 tbsp concentrated tomato purée,
   diluted in a little water or stock
Salt and pepper
A bunch of fresh basil

First, prepare the filling: heat 20 g ($\frac{2}{3}$ oz) butter and a little olive oil and sauté the pork and chicken. Crumble in the stock cube and pour in a little wine. Remove the chicken breast when it is done, mince it and transfer the meat to a bowl with the sautéed pork. Add half the Parmesan, a generous grating of nutmeg, pepper, salt and the egg, keeping back some of the white if the mixture is too moist. Mix well.

Now prepare the sauce: sauté the onion in 20 g ($\frac{2}{3}$ oz) butter and 2 tablespoons of olive oil. Add the mushrooms and the tomato purée, salt, pepper and the basil leaves. Simmer over a low heat.

Preheat the oven to 200°C (400°F, mark 6).

Boil the lasagne, a few at a time, in a large saucepanful of salted water. Drain and lay on a clean tea-towel on the table to dry. Place a little filling in the centre of each rectangle and roll up to make cannelloni.

Generously butter an oven-proof dish, lay the cannelloni in it, preferably in a single layer, and pour over the mushroom sauce. Dot with slivers of butter and sprinkle with the rest of the Par-

mesan. Finally, spread the ham over the top and bake in the oven for about 15 minutes.

Hint: In the sauce, peas may be used instead of mushrooms; add them to the sauce at the same time as the tomato purée.

Three-Coloured Cannelloni

Time: 1$\frac{3}{4}$ hours
Ingredients
450 g (1 lb) home-made or packet
   lasagne
For the filling:
100 g (3$\frac{1}{2}$ oz) cooked chicken meat
75 g (2$\frac{1}{2}$ oz) ham
30 g (1 oz) butter
60 g (2 oz) flour
350 ml (12 fl oz) milk
Salt
A little nutmeg
100 g (3$\frac{1}{2}$ oz) grated Gruyère cheese
For the sauce:
60 g (2 oz) butter
2 tbsp olive oil
$\frac{1}{2}$ onion, chopped
600 g (1$\frac{1}{4}$ lb) ripe tomatoes or
   1 225 g (8 oz) tin of peeled
   tomatoes, rubbed through a sieve
300 g (12 oz) fresh shelled, frozen or
   tinned young peas
Salt
Grated Parmesan cheese

First, prepare the filling: chop the chicken meat with the ham. In a saucepan, melt the butter and incorporate the flour. Heat the milk and add it gradually to the flour and butter. Season with salt and nutmeg and then stir in the Gruyère, chicken and ham.

Now, prepare the sauce: heat half the butter and the oil and sauté the onion. Add the tomatoes, the peas and salt. Simmer until the peas are cooked and the sauce has thickened.

Preheat the oven to 200°C (400°F, mark 6).

Boil the lasagne, a few at a time, in a large saucepanful of salted water, drain when the pasta is *al dente* and lay on a clean tea-towel to dry. Place a little filling in the centre of each rectangle and roll up to make cannelloni. Sprinkle a little of the sauce in an ovenproof dish and arrange half the cannelloni in it. Cover with some of the sauce and a little Parmesan, then make another layer of cannelloni and cover with the rest of the sauce and more Parmesan. Sprinkle slivers of the remaining butter and Parmesan over the last layer and place in the oven for about 15 minutes.

Hint: You can use leftover chicken or turkey for this filling.

Stuffed Pasta Roll with Melted Butter

Time: 2 hours
Ingredients
For the pasta:
200 g (7 oz) white or strong flour
2 eggs
Salt
For the filling:
1 kg (2¼ lb) fresh spinach or other
   greens or about 450 g (1 lb) frozen
30 g (1 oz) butter
225 g (8 oz) ricotta
30 g (1 oz) grated Parmesan cheese
Salt and pepper
For the sauce:
75 g (2½ oz) butter
A few fresh sage leaves
60 g (2 oz) grated Parmesan cheese

First, prepare the filling: wash and boil the spinach or greens. Squeeze out thoroughly, chop and mix in the butter. Leave to cool; crush the ricotta with a fork, then mix with the spinach, together with the Parmesan, salt and pepper.

Prepare the egg pasta with the ingredients listed, following the instructions on page 21. Form into a roll filled with the stuffing. Poach the roll according to the instructions on page 42 for about 40 minutes. Serve it in slices with the melted butter, sage and Parmesan.

Hint: If some of the roll is left over, arrange the slices in an ovenproof dish and cover with a very liquid béchamel sauce. Heat through in the oven. Stuffed pasta roll is also delicious with a cream and mushroom sauce.

Stuffed Pasta Roll with Melted Butter

GNOCCHI

Gnocchi are a popular Italian speciality which vary in appearance and accompanying sauces from one region to another. There are so many different types of gnocchi, and they are all good whether made with potatoes, spinach, pumpkin, carrot, cereal flours or bread and cheese.

The most commonly found variety in Italian kitchens are the gnocchi made from starchy vegetables and flour, or flour alone. They are boiled or baked in the oven, and often flavoured with eggs, cheese or greens. The dough is usually prepared on a pastry board unless, like ricotta gnocchi, it is mixed in a bowl. For the famous choux pastry gnocchi or *gnocchi alla parigina,* the dough is cooked in a saucepan directly over the heat.

Most types of gnocchi require kneading quickly and lightly, allowing the dough to retain its characteristic puffiness; if you touch it too much and heat it with your hands, it is likely to become moist and sticky.

For potato gnocchi, use a potato masher rather than a vegetable mill to obtain a purée that will not be sticky. For semolina gnocchi, you need a marble or non-absorbent slab on which to leave the dough to cool before shaping it. For gnocchi made from choux pastry, use a round-bottomed, long-handled saucepan that is not tin-plated.

Nearly all gnocchi are cooked by boiling in a large saucepanful of salted water. They are removed with the help of a slotted spoon as soon as they float to the surface and are served in layers with a great variety of different sauces.

With the more delicate types of gnocchi, like ricotta gnocchi, it is best to serve a sauce of melted butter and cheese, or cream, while for potato or other vegetable gnocchi, tomato, tomato and mushroom sauce and even meat ragù are recommended.

The recipes that follow will serve 6 as a first course or 4 as a main course.

Freshly made gnocchi and the wooden block traditionally used for shaping them

Potato Gnocchi with Tomato Sauce

Time: 1¼ hours
Ingredients
For the gnocchi:
1 kg (2¼ lb) floury potatoes
Salt
A pinch of nutmeg
About 300 g (10 oz) white flour
1 egg
For the sauce:
2 tbsp olive oil
60 g (2 oz) butter
1 small onion, chopped
1 clove garlic
500 g (1 lb 2 oz) ripe tomatoes or
    1 225 g (8 oz) tin of peeled
    tomatoes, seeded and rubbed
    through a sieve
A few fresh basil leaves
Salt
75 g (2½ oz) grated Parmesan cheese

Prepare the gnocchi: wash the potatoes and put them in a saucepan. Cover with ample cold water, add salt and boil. Drain and peel the potatoes and, while they are still hot, mash them and heap the purée on the pastry board. Add a pinch of salt and a pinch of nutmeg. Sprinkle with flour, make a well in the centre and break the egg into it; mix, adding a little more flour if necessary. You should end up with a smooth dough that no longer sticks to your hands. Do not add too much flour; it will make the gnocchi hard when cooked.

Divide the dough into pieces and roll them on the pastry board with the palms of your hands to make long sticks. Cut each stick into 2 to 3 cm (1 in) lengths and flour them. Then press them against the back of a grater or on the prongs of a fork to give them the characteristic fluted appearance. (Or you can use the little wood block specially made for the purpose.) As you make them, lay them separately on the floured pastry board.

While the potatoes are boiling, prepare the sauce: heat the oil and butter and sauté the onion with the whole clove of garlic. Add the tomatoes and the whole basil leaves. Season with salt and simmer over a low heat until the sauce thickens.

Boil the gnocchi in two or three batches in a large saucepanful of salted water, scoop them out with a slotted spoon and drain them as soon as they begin to float on the surface. Serve in layers with the sauce, from which the basil and garlic have been removed, and the Parmesan cheese.

Hint: To enrich the dish, add a few curls of butter to the gnocchi before serving.

Potato Gnocchi with Tomato Sauce

Potato Gnocchi with Mock Pesto

Time: 1½ hours
Ingredients
For the gnocchi:
1 kg (2¼ lb) floury potatoes
Salt
A pinch of nutmeg
About 300 g (10 oz) white flour
1 egg
For the sauce:
A large bunch of fresh basil
A bunch of fresh parsley
2 cloves garlic
4 tbsp grated Parmesan cheese
125 ml (4 fl oz) olive oil
Salt and pepper

Make gnocchi as described in *Potato Gnocchi with Tomato Sauce* on page 172.

Put the basil and parsley in a mortar with the garlic and cheese and grind with the pestle to form a creamy paste. Add the oil a little at a time. Season with salt and pepper.

Boil the gnocchi in a large saucepanful of salted water. Drain with a slotted spoon as soon as the gnocchi begin to float on the surface and serve with the sauce.
Hint: You can use a liquidizer instead of a pestle and mortar, and add pine nuts too, if you wish.

Potato Gnocchi Baked with Cheese

Time: 1½ hours
Ingredients
For the gnocchi:
1 kg (2¼ lb) floury potatoes
Salt
About 300 g (10 oz) white flour
1 egg
For the sauce:
200 g (7 oz) fontina cheese, thinly
   sliced
100 g (3½ oz) butter, cut into slivers
Salt

Prepare gnocchi as described in the recipe for *Potato Gnocchi with Tomato Sauce* on page 172, omitting the nutmeg.

Preheat the oven to 180°C (350°F, mark 4).

Boil the gnocchi in batches in a large saucepanful of salted water and drain with a slotted spoon as soon as they begin to float on the surface. Put them into an oven-proof dish, layering them with very thin slices of fontina and slivers of butter. Bake in the oven for about 20 minutes to melt the cheese.
Hint: Try to touch the gnocchi as little as possible with your hands while you are making them.

Semolina Gnocchi

Time: 1½ hours
Ingredients
For the gnocchi:
1 litre (1¾ pints) milk
60 g (2 oz) butter
Salt and pepper
225 g (8 oz) semolina
3 egg yolks
A little nutmeg
60 g (2 oz) grated Parmesan cheese
For the sauce:
75 g (2½ oz) butter
A few fresh sage leaves (optional)
75 g (2½ oz) grated Parmesan cheese

First make the dough for the gnocchi: heat the milk, cut the butter into pieces and add to the milk together with salt and bring to the boil. Sprinkle in the semolina steadily, stirring quickly with a wooden spoon to prevent lumps forming. Continue mixing over the heat until the mixture resembles a very thick sort of polenta.

Remove from the heat when the mixture begins to come away from the sides of the pan. Add the egg yolks, one at a time, a few pinches of nutmeg, the cheese, and pepper if you wish. Pour the mixture on to a marble slab or a smooth buttered surface, flatten it with a spatula to a thickness of about 1 cm (½ in) and leave it to cool and harden. Then, using a cutter, or a glass with a diameter of about 4 cm (1½ in), cut the dough into rounds. Dip the cutter in boiling water from time to time.

Preheat the oven to 180°C (350°F, mark 4).

Arrange the gnocchi in a buttered ovenproof dish, heaping them up a little.

For the sauce, melt the butter with the sage leaves and pour over the gnocchi. Sprinkle with cheese and bake in the oven until the gnocchi are golden brown.
Hint: This dish is also good as an accompaniment to meat roasts or stews.

Spinach and Ricotta Gnocchi

Time: 40 minutes
Ingredients
800 g (1¾ lb) spinach
250 g (9 oz) ricotta
150 g (5 oz) grated Parmesan cheese
2 eggs
Salt and pepper
A pinch of nutmeg
About 175 g (6 oz) white flour
100 g (3½ oz) butter

Clean and wash the spinach thoroughly. Drain and place in a saucepan. Cook the spinach in the water remaining on the leaves. Drain and cut into strips, then chop. Mix with the ricotta, half the Parmesan, the eggs, a pinch of salt, pepper and nutmeg and about 150 g (5 oz) of the flour to obtain a mixture that is not too moist. Flour your hands frequently and shape little balls about the size of walnuts.

Bring a large shallow pan of salted water to the boil, immerse the gnocchi, a few at a time, and remove them with a slotted spoon as they rise to the surface. Heat the butter until it is hazelnut-coloured and pour over the gnocchi with the rest of the cheese.

Hint: To prevent the mixture from being too moist, you can dry out the chopped spinach over a very low heat, before mixing it with the ricotta.

Pumpkin Gnocchi

Time: 1 hour 40 minutes
Ingredients
For the gnocchi:
1 kg (2¼ lb) pumpkin, the firm, sweet variety
A pinch of nutmeg
1 egg
About 200 g (7 oz) flour
Salt
For the sauce:
75 g (2½ oz) butter
75 g (2½ oz) grated Parmesan cheese

Cut the pumpkin into pieces, peel, discard the seeds and fibres and bake in the oven or boil in salted water until tender.

Rub the pumpkin through a sieve into a bowl and add the

nutmeg and egg. Sift in the flour a little at a time. You should obtain a fairly thick mixture.

Bring a large saucepanful of salted water to the boil. Place teaspoonfuls of the mixture in the water, immersing the spoon in the water from time to time to clean it. Work quickly and use a slotted spoon to drain the gnocchi as soon as they float to the surface. As soon as they come out of the water, pour melted butter and cheese over the gnocchi. Serve immediately.

Hint: This type of gnocchi may also be served with a simple basil and tomato sauce or with a mushroom and cream sauce.

Choux Pastry Gnocchi

Time: 1¾ hours
Ingredients
For the gnocchi:
200 ml (7 fl oz) milk
Salt
A little nutmeg
75 g (2½ oz) butter, cut into pieces
125 g (4 oz) white flour
3 eggs
2 tbsp grated Parmesan cheese
For the sauce:
100 g (3½ oz) butter
40 g (1½ oz) flour
½ litre (18 fl oz) milk, heated
Salt
100 g (3½ oz) grated Parmesan cheese

Prepare the gnocchi dough first: pour the milk into a saucepan with a few pinches of salt and nutmeg and the butter. Bring to the boil. Remove the saucepan from the heat for a moment and pour in the flour all at once, stirring vigorously with a wooden spoon to stop lumps forming. Replace the pan over the heat and continue stirring until the dough is dry and comes away from the sides of the saucepan. It should make a slight noise as if it were being fried. Off the heat, allow to cool, stirring frequently and incorporating the eggs, one at a time. If the dough is too firm, add a fourth egg. Finally, add the cheese and work the dough for 10 minutes.

Meanwhile, bring a large pan of salted water to the boil. Put the dough in a cloth piping bag with a plain nozzle about 1 cm ($\frac{1}{2}$ in) in diameter. Squeeze the bag to produce a cylinder of dough about 2.5 cm (1 in) long and drop it straight into the boiling water, using a knife to cut off the dough cleanly. Turn the heat down as low as possible. Continue until you have used up all the dough, dipping the knife in the water from time to time. Boil the gnocchi for 8 to 9 minutes. Drain with a slotted spoon and place on a clean tea-towel to dry.

To make the sauce, melt 40 g (1$\frac{1}{2}$ oz) of the butter in a saucepan. Add the flour and stir then add the hot milk, a little at a time. Season with salt and let the sauce thicken. Remove from the heat and add half the cheese.

Preheat the oven to 180°C (350°F, mark 4).

Arrange the gnocchi in a buttered ovenproof dish. Melt the remaining butter and pour some over the gnocchi, then pour over about two-thirds of the béchamel sauce. Sprinkle a little grated cheese over and mix all together carefully. Spread the gnocchi out and pour over the rest of the sauce, the rest of the melted butter and the rest of the cheese. Place in the oven for 10 minutes then turn the oven up to 190°-200°C (375°-400°F, mark 5 to 6) and leave for a further 10 minutes.

Serve when the gnocchi are nice and puffy, straight from the oven, in the same dish.

Hint: The size of the eggs used does not matter, as you can always add another one if necessary. The gnocchi can also be served with a sauce based on butter, creamy soft Gorgonzola and mascherpone cheeses.

PANCAKES

Pancakes or crêpes are made from a batter of milk, flour and eggs which is fried paper-thin and stuffed with various fillings based on either meat, spinach and ricotta or other vegetable mixtures. Once they are filled, they can be rolled up, folded in four, or stacked one on top of the other to make a kind of layered cake. Finally, they are covered with smooth béchamel sauce and baked in the oven. Pancakes are usually served as a main course.

To make pancakes, you need a small frying pan about 15 cm (6 in) in diameter with a long handle, or a non-stick pan which makes it possible to make pancakes without additional fat. The cooking process is simplified if you use an electric pancake maker. These are equipped with a round plate on to which the runny pancake batter is poured. A very hot hotplate is pressed down on top of it. After it has been turned over and the lid opened the mixture on the hotplate is paper-thin and cooked.

To obtain very thin pancakes, the batter should be fairly runny so that it will spread easily and evenly over the bottom of the frying pan. The pan should be placed over a medium heat so that the batter will stick immediately but without burning. If you use an iron pan, it is advisable to keep shaking the pan with a circular motion to help the mixture spread rapidly.

To make pancakes for four people, use 4 eggs to 100 g (3½ oz) white flour, a pinch of salt and about 150 ml (5 fl oz) milk or water. It is customary to leave the batter to rest before making the pancakes, for anything between half an hour and several hours. This enables the ingredients to combine and makes the batter more elastic.

Pancakes can also be stored in the freezer for several months. If you are freezing pancakes in a béchamel sauce use very little butter; you can always add slivers of butter when you bake the dish in the oven. Take the pancakes out of the freezer well in advance to enable them to thaw properly.

The recipes that follow will serve 6 as a first course or 4 as a main course.

Pancakes filled with spinach and pine nuts ready for finishing in the oven

The Priest's Housekeeper's Pancakes

Time: 1½ hours
Ingredients
For the pancakes:
4 eggs
Salt
100 g (3½ oz) white flour
150 ml (5 fl oz) milk
A knob of butter or lard
For the filling:
½ small onion, chopped
A knob of butter
1 chicken liver, chopped into small
  pieces
100 g (3½ oz) sweetbreads, chopped
  into small pieces
Salt
100 g (3½ oz) ham
300 g (10 oz) spinach, boiled,
  drained and chopped
150 g (5 oz) ricotta
1 egg
60 g (2 oz) grated Parmesan cheese
A little nutmeg
For the sauce:
60 g (2 oz) butter
40 g (1½ oz) flour
½ litre (18 fl oz) milk, heated
Salt
60 g (2 oz) grated Parmesan cheese

First, make the pancakes: beat the eggs in a bowl with a pinch of salt. Add the flour and mix thoroughly to obtain a smooth mixture with no lumps. Add the milk, a little at a time, stirring constantly. You should end up with a fairly runny mixture. Cover with a plate and leave to rest for at least 30 minutes. Melt the knob of butter in an iron or non-stick long-handled frying pan and heat. When the pan is hot, pour in a ladleful of the pancake batter, shaking the pan from side to side with a circular motion so that the mixture forms a thin, even layer on the bottom of the pan. As soon as the pancake has formed, toss it and cook the other side. Remove each pancake as you make it and keep it warm. Continue making pancakes in this way until the batter is used up.

Now prepare the filling: fry the onion in the butter and add the chicken liver, sweetbreads and salt and sauté for a few minutes. Transfer to a bowl and finely chop with the ham. Mix in the spinach, ricotta, egg, Parmesan, grated nutmeg and salt.

At this point, prepare the béchamel sauce: melt 40 g (1½ oz) of the butter in a saucepan and incorporate the flour. Stir well to eliminate any lumps and pour in the hot milk a little at a time. Add salt and half the Parmesan.

Preheat the oven to 190°C (375°F, mark 5).

Place some filling in the centre of each pancake and roll them up. Pour a little béchamel sauce into an ovenproof dish and arrange the pancakes in it. Pour over the rest of the béchamel and sprinkle with Parmesan and the remaining butter cut into slivers. Bake in the oven for 10 to 15 minutes. Serve from the same dish.

Hint: To avoid the formation of lumps in the pancake mixture, break in the eggs one at a time and incorporate a tablespoon or so of flour between each egg until all the eggs and flour have been mixed in. Then add the milk.

Pancakes 'Miriam'

Time: 1½ hours
Ingredients
For the pancakes:
4 eggs
Salt
100 g (3½ oz) flour
150 ml (5 fl oz) milk
A knob of butter or lard
For the filling and sauce:
200 g (7 oz) calf's brain and marrow
100 g (3½ oz) chicken livers, cleaned
1 clove garlic
A handful of parsley, chopped
60 g (2 oz) butter
2 tbsp olive oil
A little dry Marsala
1 tsp concentrated tomato purée,
    diluted with a little water
Salt and pepper
40 g (1½ oz) flour
½ litre (18 fl oz) milk, heated
A little nutmeg
30 g (1 oz) grated Parmesan cheese
1 egg yolk

Prepare and cook the pancakes as described for *Priest's House-keeper's Pancakes* on page 180.

Blanch the brains and marrow in boiling water for a few seconds. Drain and chop together with the chicken livers. Brown the whole clove of garlic and the parsley in 20 g (⅔ oz) of the butter and the oil. Add the mixed meats and cook over a high heat for a few minutes. Pour over a little Marsala and add the tomato purée and continue simmering for a few minutes. Finally, add salt, pepper and remove from the heat.

Melt the remaining butter except for a knob in a saucepan and stir in the flour. Mix well to eliminate any lumps. Dilute with the hot milk, poured in a little at a time, and stir constantly. You should obtain a smooth béchamel sauce. Season with salt, pepper and nutmeg. Add the Parmesan and, with the pan off the heat, the egg yolk.

Preheat the oven to 180°C (350°F, mark 4).

Mix half the béchamel with the meat mixture and place a little in the centre of each pancake. Roll them up and place them side by side in a buttered ovenproof dish. Pour the rest of the béchamel on top and bake in the oven until a gratin topping forms.

Hint: As this is a very rich dish serve it with light accompaniments such as a tossed green salad.

Pancakes with Mushrooms

Time: 1¼ hours
Ingredients
For the pancakes:
4 eggs
Salt
100 g (3½ oz) flour
150 ml (5 fl oz) milk
A knob of butter or lard
For the filling and sauce:
300 g (10 oz) fresh mushrooms,
   cleaned and thinly sliced
100 g (3½ oz) butter
Salt
1 tbsp flour
250 ml (9 fl oz) milk, heated
A little nutmeg
100 g (3½ oz) ham, chopped

Prepare and cook the pancakes as described in *Priest's House- keeper's Pancakes* on page 180.

Sauté the mushrooms in 30 g (1 oz) of the butter with a pinch of salt. In another saucepan, melt 30 g (1 oz) of the butter and stir in the flour. Dilute with the hot milk, poured in a little at a time, and stir constantly. Season with salt and nutmeg and cook for 5 minutes. Remove from the heat and add the ham and mushrooms.

Preheat the oven to 180°C (350°F, mark 4).

Place some filling in the centre of each pancake and roll them up. Arrange them in a buttered oven- proof dish and pour over the remaining butter, melted. Bake in the oven for a few minutes.

Hint: To enhance the flavour of the sauce, rub a few of the mush- rooms through a sieve. You can also use dried ceps for this sauce (soaked in warm water and then drained).

Pancakes with Ham

Time: 1 hour
Ingredients
For the pancakes:
4 eggs
Salt
100 g (3½ oz) flour
150 ml (5 fl oz) milk
A knob of butter or lard
For the filling and sauce:
60 g (2 oz) butter
1 tbsp flour
250 ml (9 fl oz) milk, heated
Salt and pepper
A little nutmeg
2 tbsp grated Parmesan cheese
1 egg yolk
200 g (7 oz) fontina (or other good
   melting cheese) in slices
150 g (5 oz) ham, sliced

Prepare and cook the pancakes as described in *Priest's House- keeper's Pancakes* on page 180.

Melt 30 g (1 oz) of the butter in a saucepan and stir in the flour. Mix well and dilute with the hot milk, poured in a little at a time, and stir constantly. Season with salt, pepper and nutmeg. Simmer the sauce for 5 minutes. Remove the pan from the heat and stir in the Parmesan and egg yolk.

Preheat the oven to 180°C (350°F, mark 4).

Place a slice of fontina and then a slice of ham on each pancake. Roll them up and arrange in a buttered ovenproof dish. Pour over the béchamel and scatter slivers of butter on top. Bake in the oven for a few minutes.

Hint: For a stronger flavour, use slices of Würstel instead of ham.

Very Refined Pancakes

Time: 1½ hours
Ingredients
For the pancakes:
4 eggs
Salt
100 g (3½ oz) flour
150 ml (5 fl oz) milk
A knob of butter or lard
For the filling and sauce:
1 small piece of onion, chopped
75 g (2½ oz) butter
200 g (7 oz) minced pork
200 g (7 oz) lean minced beef
20 g (⅔ oz) dried cep mushrooms, soaked, drained and sliced
Salt and pepper
About 250 ml (9 fl oz) stock, heated
30 g (1 oz) flour
1 small black truffle (optional), grated
1 mozzarella cheese, chopped
A little nutmeg

Prepare the pancakes as described for *Priest's Housekeeper's Pancakes* on page 180.

To make the filling, sauté the onion in 30 g (1 oz) of the butter and add the minced pork and beef, the mushrooms and salt. Simmer, adding 1 to 2 tablespoons of stock if necessary.

Meanwhile, melt 30 g (1 oz) of the butter in another saucepan and stir in the flour. Mix well and dilute with the boiling stock, poured in a little at a time. Cook the sauce for a few minutes then stir in a few tablespoons of the meat mixture, a little truffle and the mozzarella; season with salt, pepper and nutmeg.

Preheat the oven to 180°C (350°F, mark 4).

Fill the pancakes, roll them up and arrange them in a buttered ovenproof dish. Pour over the sauce and scatter slivers of truffle and butter over the top. Bake in the oven for a few minutes.

Hint: Serve this with a mixed raw vegetable salad with a dressing of olive oil, salt and pepper.

Pancakes with Asparagus

Time: 1½ hours
Ingredients
For the pancakes:
4 eggs
Salt
100 g (3½ oz) flour
150 ml (5 fl oz) milk
A knob of butter or lard
For the filling and sauce:
A bunch of asparagus weighing about 800 g (1¾ lb)

90 g (3 oz) butter
Salt and pepper
60 g (2 oz) flour
400 ml (14 fl oz) milk, heated
A little nutmeg
60 g (2 oz) grated Parmesan cheese
100 g (3½ oz) Gruyère cheese, thinly
   sliced

Prepare and cook the pancakes as described for *Priest's House-keeper's Pancakes* on page 180.

To make the filling, boil the asparagus (or, preferably, steam them), remove the stalks and the hardest green part and sauté the tips with 30 g (1 oz) of the butter and a pinch of salt. Then, rub through a sieve.

Prepare a fairly thick béchamel sauce by melting the rest of the butter and stirring in the flour and the hot milk. Season with salt, pepper and nutmeg and cook for 5 minutes. Keep about a quarter of the sauce back and mix the asparagus purée with the rest, together with the Parmesan.

Preheat the oven to 180°C (350°F, mark 4).

Spread the mixture on the pancakes, placing a slice of Gruyère on each. Roll the pancakes up and arrange them in a buttered ovenproof dish. Spread over the rest of the béchamel and bake in the oven for a few minutes.

Hint: Out of season, you can use frozen asparagus tips.

Gorgonzola Pancakes

Time: 1 hour
Ingredients
For the pancakes:
4 eggs
Salt
100 g (3½ oz) flour
150 ml (5 fl oz) milk
A knob of butter or lard
For the filling and sauce:
75 g (2½ oz) butter
1 tbsp flour
250 ml (9 fl oz) milk, heated
Salt and pepper
A little nutmeg
150 g (5 oz) mild Gorgonzola
   cheese, cut into pieces
60 g (2 oz) grated Parmesan cheese

Prepare and cook the pancakes as described on page 180.

Melt 30 g (1 oz) of the butter in a saucepan and stir in the flour. Dilute with the hot milk and stir constantly. Add salt, pepper and nutmeg and cook for 5 minutes. Remove from the heat and stir in the Gorgonzola and half the Parmesan.

Preheat the oven to 180°C (350°F, mark 4).

Fill the pancakes and roll them up. Arrange them in a buttered ovenproof dish. Pour over the remaining butter, melted, and sprinkle with the rest of the Parmesan. Bake for a few minutes.

Hint: If you are cooking for children, use grated Emmenthal instead of Gorgonzola.

Gorgonzola Pancakes

184

INDEX

Page numbers in *italic* refer to illustrations

Agnolini, 34, 36, 149
Agnolotti, 149
  to prepare, 34, 36
  Agnolotti with Tomato Sauce, *33*
  Tasty Agnolotti, 150, *151*
Anchovy
  Maccheroni with Mozzarella and
    Anchovies, 94, *95*
  Wholewheat Spaghetti with Anchovy
    and Capers, 112
Artichokes: with Ceriole, *90*, 91
Asparagus: with Pancakes, 183-4
Aubergine
  Ditaloni with Aubergines, 100
  Spaghetti with Aubergine and Sweet
    Pepper Sauce, 88, *89*, 90
Avemarie (pasta), 57

Bacon
  Garganelli with Bacon Sauce, 70-1
  Spaghetti with Bacon, 66, *67*
Baked Maccheroni, 106, *107*
Baked Pasta-Filled Tomatoes, 98, *99*, 100
Basil
  Fazzoletti with Basil Cream Sauce, 104
  Fettuccine with Basil-Flavoured
    Sauce, 75-6
  Home-Made Lasagne with Basil
    Sauce, 104-5
  Spaghetti with Marrow Flowers and
    Basil, 112, *113*
  Trofie with Basil Sauce, 110, *111*
Béchamel sauce, 131
Bigoli, 45, 58
Bolognese sauce
  to freeze, 62
  Cappelletti with Bolognese Sauce,
    156-7
  Fettuccine with Bolognese Sauce, 75
  Green Lasagne with Bolognese Sauce,
    84
Bucatini, 57
  Bucatini with Hake, 118, 120

Bucatini alla Marinara, 120
Bucatini with Prawns and Clams, 124,
  125, 126

Calzoncini, 36
Calzoni, 149
Cannelloni, *148*
  to freeze, 62
  to prepare and serve, 36, 149
  Cannelloni Filled with Chicken, 165-6
  Cannelloni with Mascherpone, *41*, 165
  Cannelloni Simona, 166-7
  Three-Coloured Cannelloni, 167-8
Cannolicchi with Ham and Tomato
  Sauce, 96, *97*
Capelli d'angelo, 57
Capers
  Ruote with Olives and Capers, 101
  Wholewheat Spaghetti with Anchovy
    and Capers, 112
Cappelletti, *148*, 149
  to prepare and serve, 42, 45
  Cappelletti with Bolognese Sauce,
    156-7
  Cappelletti with Mushroom Sauce,
    154, *155*, 156
  Cappelletti Pie, 157-8
Cappieddi: Home-Made with Mushroom
  Sauce, 108
Casonsei
  to prepare and serve, 36
  Casonsei Brescia-Style, 159
  with Pumpkin and Pheasant, 160
Cavatieddi, 58
Caviare: with Tagliolini, 127-8
Ceriole, *44*
  to prepare and serve, 49-50
  Ceriole with Artichokes, 90, *91*
Cheese, *see also* Gorgonzola, Gruyère,
    Mascherpone, Mozzarella, Ricotta
  Conchiglie with Creamy Cheese
    Sauce, 142
  Pasta Piena with Cheese Sauce, 164-5
  Potato Gnocchi Baked with Cheese,
    174

Tagliatelle with Cheesy Onion Sauce,
  101
Chicken, Cannelloni Filled with, 165-6
Chilli: with Penne, 94
Choux Pastry Gnocchi, 171, 176-7
Clams: with Bucatini and Prawns, 124,
  125, 126
Cold Ruote with Tomato Sauce, 100-1
Cold Summer Spaghetti, 90
Coloured pasta, 27, *28*, 29-32
Conchiglie
  Conchiglie with Creamy Cheese
    Sauce, 142
  Conchiglie with Würstel, 69-70
Cooking pasta, 53, 54-5
Corzetti, 46
Courgette Sauce: with Trenette, 98
Crab Sauce, Sedanini in, 143
Curry Sauce: with Tagliatelle and Lamb,
  74
Cuttlefish: with Spaghetti, 121-2

Ditalini, 57
Ditaloni with Aubergines, 100
Dough for pasta
  to cut, 25-7
  to mix, 23-4
  to roll, 24

Eels: with Fusilli, 118, *119*

Farfalle, *20*, 26
Farfalloni, Spicy, with Walnuts, 142
Farmhouse-Style Penne, 136, *137*
Fazzoletti with Basil Cream Sauce, 104
Fettuccine, *20*
  to prepare and serve, 25
  sauces for, 57
  Fettuccine with Basil-Flavoured
    Sauce, 75-6
  Fettuccine with Bolognese Sauce, 75
  Fettuccine with Lamb Sauce, 76, *77*
  Fettuccine with Truffle, 146, *147*
Fish sauces, *116*, 117-29; *see also* Clam,
  Crab, Mussel, etc.
Four-Flavoured Spaghetti, 132

Freezing pasta, 59-60, *61*, 62-4
Fusilli
    Fusilli with Eels, 118, *119*
    Fusilli Hunter's-Style, 80-1
    Fusilli with Sausage and Mushroom
        Ragù, 66

Galani, 26
Garganelli
    to prepare and serve, 46
    Garganelli with Bacon Sauce, *47*,
        70-1
Garlic: with Maccheroni, Oil and
    Parsley, 114, *115*
Gnocchi, *170*, 171
    Choux Pastry Gnocchi, 171, 176-7
    Potato Gnocchi Baked with Cheese,
        174
    Potato Gnocchi with Mock Pesto, 174
    Potato Gnocchi with Tomato Sauce,
        172, *173*
    Pumpkin Gnocchi, 176
    Semolina Gnocchi, 175
Gobbetti, 57
Gorgonzola Pancakes, 184, *185*
Green Lasagne with Bolognese Sauce, 84
Green Tagliatelle with Mushrooms and
    Peas, 103
Gruyère: with Maccheroni, 134, 136

Hake: with Bucatini, 118, 120
Ham
    Cannolicchi with Ham and Tomato
        Sauce, 96, *97*
    Pancakes with Ham, 182-3
Hare: with Pappardelle, 8, *79*, 80
Home-Made Cappieddi with Mushroom
    Sauce, 108
Home-Made Lasagne with Basil Sauce,
    104-5
Home-made pasta, 21-51, *43*
    to cut shapes, 25-7
    ingredients, *20*, 22-3
    to mix and roll dough, 23-4
    pasta-making machines, 21-2, 24
    utensils, 21

Ingredients for pasta, *20*, 22-3
Italian-Style Orecchiette with Ragù, 72,
    73, 74

Lagane
    to prepare and serve, 25
    sauces for, 57
Laganelle
    to prepare and serve, 25
    sauces for, 57
    Laganelle with Walnut and Pine
        Sauce, 134, *135*
Lamb
    Fettuccine with Lamb Sauce, 76, *77*
    Tagliatelle with Lamb and Curry
        Sauce, 74-5
Lasagne
    to freeze, 62, 63
    to prepare and serve, 26
    sauces for, 57
    Green Lasagne with Bolognese Sauce,
        84
    Home-Made Lasagne with Basil
        Sauce, 104-5
    Lasagne with Meat Balls, 84-5
    Two-Filling Lasagne Pie, 83
Lasagnette, 57
Linguine
    to prepare and serve, 25
    sauces for, 57
    Linguine 'Mimosa', 132, 134
    Linguine with Mussel Sauce, 122, 124

Maccaruni, 48
Maccheroni
    to prepare and serve, 48
    sauces for, 58
    Baked Maccheroni, 106, *107*
    Maccheroni Baked in Foil, 92
    with Garlic, Oil and Parsley, 114, *115*
    Maccheroni with Gruyère, 134, 136
    Maccheroni with Meat Ball Ragù, 69
    Maccheroni with Mozzarella and
        Anchovies, 94, *95*
    Maccheroni with Olives, 92, *93*
    Maccheroni with Prawns, 126

Maccheroni with Sardines, 128, *129*
Malloreddus, *44*
    to prepare and serve, 48
    sauces for, 58
    with Tomato Sauce, 108, *109*, 110
Maltagliati
    to prepare and serve, 25
    Maltagliati with Ragù, 66, 68
    Tasty Maltagliati Pie, 81
Maritime Spaghetti, 120-1
Marrow
    Marrow Tortelli, 158-9
    Rigatoni with Marrow, 140, *141*
    Spaghetti with Marrow Flowers and
        Basil, 112, *113*
Marubini
    to prepare and serve, 36, 38
    Marubini with Financière Sauce, 161
Mascherpone: with Cannelloni, *41*, 165
Meat balls
    Lasagne with Meat Balls, 84-5
    Maccheroni with Meat Ball Ragù, 69
Mezze maniche, 57
'Mimosa' Linguine, 132, 134
Mozzarella
    Maccheroni with Mozzarella and
        Anchovies, 94, *95*
Mushrooms, 29
    Cappelletti with Mushroom Sauce,
        154, *155*, 156
    Fusilli with Sausage and Mushroom
        Ragù, 66
    Home-Made Cappieddi with
        Mushroom Sauce, 108
    Pancakes with Mushrooms, 182
    Tagliatelle with Mushrooms and Peas,
        103-4
Mussels
    Linguine with Mussel Sauce, 122, 124
    Spaghetti with Tiny Mussels, 122, *123*

Nodini, 26

Ofelle
    to prepare and serve, 38
    Ofelle Trieste-Style, 162

Olives
   Maccheroni with Olives, 92, *93*
   Ruote with Olives and Capers, 101
Onion
   Tagliatelle with Cheesy Onion Sauce,
     101, 103
   Tagliatelle with Onion Sauce, 105
Orecchiette, *44*
   to prepare and serve, 49
   sauces for, 58
   Italian-Style Orecchiette with Ragù,
     72, *73*, 74
   Orecchiette with Veal and Pork Rolls,
     72

Pancakes, *178*, 179-85
   Gorgonzola Pancakes, 184, *185*
   Pancakes with Asparagus, 183-4
   Pancakes with Ham, 182-3
   Pancakes 'Miriam', 181
   Pancakes with Mushrooms, 182
   The Priest's Housekeeper's Pancakes,
     180-1
   Very Refined Pancakes, 183
Panciuti, *44*
   to prepare and serve, 38, 39, 40
   Panciuti 'al Preboggion', 162, *163*, 164
   Panciuti with Melted Butter and
     Cheese, *39*
Pansoti, 38, 40
Pappardelle
   to prepare and serve, 26
   sauces for, 57
   Pappardelle au Gratin, 76, 78
   Pappardelle with Hare, 78, *79*, 80
   Superlative Pappardelle, 143-4
Parsley: with Maccheroni, Garlic and
   Oil, 114, *115*
Pasta Grattugiata, 27
Pasta-making machines, 21-2, 24
Pasta piena
   to prepare and serve, 40
   Pasta Piena with Cheese Sauce, 164-5
Pasta Tritata, 27
Peas: with Tagliatelle and Mushrooms,
   103-4

Penne
   sauces for, 57
   Farmhouse-Style Penne, 136, *137*
   Penne with Chilli, 94
   Penne with Pork Ragù, 68
   Penne with Salami, 138, *139*
   Penne with Smoked Salmon, 127
   Penne with Würstel, 138
Pepper: Spaghetti with Aubergine and
   Sweet Pepper Sauce, 88, *89*, 90
Pheasant: with Casonsei and Pumpkin,
   160
Pie
   Cappelletti Pie, 157-8
   Tasty Maltagliati Pie, 81
   Two-Filling Lasagne Pie, 83
Pizzocheri, 49, 58
Pork
   Orecchiette with Veal and Pork Rolls,
     72
   Penne with Pork Ragù, 68
Potato gnocchi, 171
   Potato Gnocchi Baked with Cheese,
     174
   Potato Gnocchi with Mock Pesto, 174
   Potato Gnocchi with Tomato Sauce,
     172, *173*
Prawn
   Bucatini with Clams and Prawns, 124,
     125, 126
   Maccheroni with Prawns, 126
Pumpkin, 29
   Casonsei with Pumpkin and Pheasant,
     160
   Pumpkin Gnocchi, 176

Quadrettini, *20*
Quadrucci, 26

Ragù (meat sauce), 57-8, 64-86
   ingredients, *64*, 65
   Fusilli with Sausage and Mushroom
     Ragù, 66
   Italian-Style Orecchiette with Ragù,
     72, *73*, 74
   Maccheroni with Meat Ball Ragù, 69

   Maltagliati with Ragù, 66, 68
   Penne with Pork Ragù, 68
   Ravioli with Marrow Filling and
     Ragù, *37*
Ravioli, 149
   to prepare and serve, 40
   Ravioli with Marrow Filling and
     Ragù, *37*
   Ravioli with Melted Butter, 150, 152
   Ravioli Stuffed with Spinach and
     Ricotta, 152, *153*, 154
Reginette, 26
Regional varieties of pasta, 45-51
Ricotta, 171
   Ravioli Stuffed with Spinach and
     Ricotta, 152, *153*, 154
   Spinach and Ricotta Gnocchi, 175-6
Rigatoni
   Rigatoni with Aromatic Herbs, 96
   Rigatoni 'In the Pink', 138, 140
   Rigatoni with Marrow, 140, *141*
Rosemary: with Spaghetti, 88
Rotolo, 42, 62, 149
Ruote
   Cold Ruote with Tomato Sauce, 100-1
   Ruote with Olives and Capers, 101

Salami: with Penne, 138, *139*
Salmon, Smoked, with Penne, 127
Sardines: with Maccheroni, 128, *129*
Sauces, *52*, 53, 57-8, *64*, 65, *86*, 87, *116*,
   117, *130*, 131
   aubergine and sweet pepper sauce, 88,
     89, 90
   bacon sauce, 70-1
   basil sauce, 75-6, 104-5, 110, *111*
   béchamel (white) sauce, *130*, 131
   bolognese sauce, 62, 75, 84, 156-7
   cheese sauce, 142, 164-5
   courgette sauce, 98
   crab sauce, 143
   financière sauce, 161
   ham and tomato sauce, 96, *97*
   lamb and curry sauce, 74-5
   lamb sauce, 76, *77*
   mushroom sauce, 108, 154, *155*, 156

mussel sauce, 122, 124
onion sauce, 101, 103, 105
tomato and herb sauce, *102*, 103
tomato sauce, 100-1, 108, *109*, 110,
    172, *173*
walnut and pine sauce, 134, *135*
white (béchamel) sauce, *130*, 131
Sausage
   Fusilli with Sausage and Mushroom
      Ragù, 66
   Torciglioni with Sausages, 70, *71*
Sedanini
   sauces for, 57
   Sedanini in Crab Sauce, 143
   Truffled Sedanini, 142-3
Semolina Gnocchi, 175
Serving pasta, 56
Soufflé, Tagliatelle, 105-6
Spaghetti
   to freeze, 62, 63
   sauces for, 57
   Cold Summer Spaghetti, 90
   Four-Flavoured Spaghetti, 132
   Maritime Spaghetti, 120-1
   Spaghetti with Aubergine and Sweet
      Pepper Sauce, 88, *89*, 90
   Spaghetti with Bacon, 66, *67*
   Spaghetti 'Buried in Sand', 132, *133*
   Spaghetti with Cuttlefish, 121-2
   Spaghetti with Marrow Flowers and
      Basil, 112, *113*
   Spaghetti with Rosemary, 88
   Spaghetti with Tiny Mussels, 122, *123*
   Wholewheat Spaghetti with Anchovy
      and Capers, 112
   Wholewheat Spaghetti with Vegetable
      Sauce, 110, 112
Spicy Farfalloni with Walnuts, 142
Spinach, 27
   in pancakes, *178*
   Ravioli Stuffed with Spinach and
      Ricotta, 152, *153*, 154
   Spinach and Ricotta Gnocchi, 175-6
Strangolapreti, 50
Strasciati, strascinati, 49
Stringozzi, 49-50

Strozzapreti, 50
Stuffed pasta, 32-45, *43*, *148*, 149
   Stuffed Pasta Roll, 168, *169*
Superlative Pappardelle, 143-4

Tagliatelle
   to prepare and serve, 25
   sauces for, 57
   Green Tagliatelle with Mushrooms
      and Peas, 103-4
   Tagliatelle with Cheesy Onion Sauce,
      101, 103
   Tagliatelle with Lamb and Curry
      Sauce, 74-5
   Tagliatelle with Onion Sauce, 105
   Tagliatelle Soufflé, 105-6
   Tagliatelle with Tomato and Herb
      Sauce, *102*, 103
   Tagliatelle with Triple Butter Sauce,
      144, *145*, 146
   Tagliatelle with Veal Kebabs, 81-2
Tagliatelline, *20*
Taglierini, 25
Tagliolini
   to prepare and serve, 25
   Tagliolini with Caviare, 127-8
Tasty Agnolotti, 150, *151*
Tasty Maltagliati Pie, 81
Three-Coloured Cannelloni, 167
Tomato, 30, 31
   Baked Pasta-Filled Tomatoes, 98, *99*,
      100
   Cannolicchi with Ham and Tomato
      Sauce, 96, 97
   Cold Ruote with Tomato Sauce, 100-1
   Malloreddus with Tomato Sauce, 108,
      109, 110
   Potato Gnocchi with Tomato Sauce,
      172, *173*
   Tagliatelle with Tomato and Herb
      Sauce, *102*, 103
Torciglioni
   sauces for, 57
   Torciglioni with Sausages, 70, *71*
   Torciglioni with Tuna, 126-7

Tortelli
   to prepare and serve, 42
   Marrow Tortelli, 158-9
Tortellini
   to prepare and serve, 42, 45
   Tortellini in Cream with Vol-au-Vent,
      35
Trenette
   sauces for, 57
   Trenette with Courgette Sauce, 98
Trofie, *44*
   to prepare and serve, 50-1
   Trofie with Basil Sauce, 110, *111*
Truffle
   Fettuccine with Truffle, 146, *147*
   Truffled Sedanini, 142-3
Tuna, with Torciglioni, 126-7
Two-Filling Lasagne Pie, 83

Veal
   Orecchiette with Veal and Pork Rolls,
      72
   Tagliatelle with Veal Kebabs, 81-2
Vegetable sauces, *86*, 87-115; *see also*
      Asparagus, Spinach, Tomato, etc.
Vermicelli, 57
Very Refined Pancakes, 183
Viti, 57

Walnuts: with Spicy Farfalloni, 142
White sauces, 130, 131-47
Wholewheat pasta
   Wholewheat Spaghetti with Anchovy
      and Capers, 112
   Wholewheat Spaghetti with Vegetable
      Sauce, 110, 112
Wine and pasta, 8-9
Würstel
   Conchiglie with Würstel, 69-70
   Penne with Würstel, 138, *139*

Zite, 57
Zitoni, 57

LUIGI VERONELLI

Born in Milan in 1926, Luigi Veronelli is one of the best-known food writers in Italy. He studied classics and philosophy before working in commerce, and later turned to writing and journalism, specializing in the culinary arts. He is the author of many books on food and cookery, and has presented three major television series in Italy. He has contributed to several respected newspapers and periodicals, including *Il Giorno, L'Espresso* and *Il Vino*. He has also devoted a considerable amount of his time to the study of wine, and has been responsible for several important reference works on the wines of Italy and of the world.

SIMONETTA LUPI VADA

Simonetta Lupi Vada began her career in 1958 as an editor for *Cucina Italiana,* Italy's first and foremost cooking magazine. Since then she has edited numerous food and cookery books and has written many of her own recipes. She also writes a monthly column on cooking and nutrition for the Italian magazine *Benissimo,* and has been a food consultant for several major Italian companies.